Daily Seed

A Bitcoiner's Devotional

Daniel Howell

Blue Ridge Books, LLC

Copyright © 2024 Daniel Howell

Blue Ridge Books, LLC
PO Box 4652
Lynchburg, VA 24502
www.BlueRidgeBooks.net

ISBN 978-0-9987481-2-2

9 780998 748122   90000

Published July 2024 at block height 850,500

Printed in the United States of America

9 8 7 6 5 4 3 2 1   First Edition   10 11 12 13 14

PREFACE

Most of us take little notice of plants. We see the grass, flowers, bushes, and trees, but they are usually just the backdrop to our world rather than the object of our attention. However, plants are amazing creatures. Without moving, they spread to cover the Earth. Using the wind and animals, they cast their seeds far and wide via pollen, nuts, or even fruit.

Although seeds are small enough to hold in your hand, they contain all the information needed – in the right environment – to regenerate the entire plant, even towering and majestic redwood trees. Because of this awesome potential, seeds are often spoken of metaphorically. Even Jesus spoke of seeds this way in his parables.

In Bitcoin, the word *seed* is used in reference to a private key. With just a private key, you can recreate an entire bitcoin wallet, including the public key and all addresses used to send and receive bitcoins.

A bitcoin wallet on your phone or computer uses public / private key cryptography. The public key is used to derive addresses for sending and receiving bitcoin payments. As the name implies, a public key can be shared publicly. The private key is used to sign bitcoin transactions, proving you own the coins you wish to spend or move. The private key must not be shared because anyone with knowledge of your private key can send (i.e., steal) your coins.

Private keys are long, hexadecimal numbers. They are great for computers but terrible for people. Making a hand copy of a private key is almost guaranteed to lead to mistakes and lost bitcoins. (You never want to make an electronic copy of a private key). To make backing up private keys easier, a proposal[1] was adopted by wallet makers to convert the private key into a list of 12 or 24 words. These words are called a *seed phrase or seed words*. They are easy for humans to memorize or write down and save in a safe place. You can also add a 13th (or 25th) word, called a passphrase, for added security. The passphrase can be letters, numbers, or entire sentences. In this devotional, a verse of the day is presented as a 12- or 24-word seed phrase, sometimes with a passphrase.

---

[1] BIP-39, or Bitcoin Improvement Proposal #39

Every wallet has a name and a fingerprint. In this devotional, the date serves as our wallet name and the page number is the fingerprint. Wallets also have a derivation path used to locate your coins. The derivation path usually looks something like m/84'/0'/0'. In this devotional, the derivation path is the Scripture verse being cited that day, e.g., nt/john/3/16. An "nt" in the path stands for New Testament, "ot" stands for Old Testament.

The Daily Seed orange pill ( ) was inspired by the good folks at SeedSigner. A SeedSigner is a small computer you can build yourself to sign bitcoin transactions, or you can purchase one pre-built from seedsigner.com. To sign a transaction, you first import your seed words into the device. To make this faster, easier, and error-proof, you can convert your seed words into a QR code which the device can scan to quickly import your words. In this book, a QR code is provided with the seed words each day. You can scan this code to read a short devotional related to the verse of the day. If your phone doesn't have a QR code scanner, or if your scanner doesn't decode the devotional text properly, try any number of free QR code readers available in your app store.

It likely goes without saying, but most of the verses in this devotional have been modified to fit into 12 or 24 words. That is, they are not quoted directly from the Scriptures. I believe the changes are benign, but you should be aware that verses may not be canonical.

I pray you enjoy this devotional and find it inspiring. The seed words found on these pages may not be actual BIP-39 words, but they are better. They are the wise words of our God and Savior meant to lead us along the path of righteous living. May these seed words be planted in your heart and produce every good fruit of the Spirit in your life.

PS. Never create an actual wallet from seed words that make a readable phrase, such as a Scripture verse. Such wallets are not random, and your coins will be stolen. Always have a software wallet generate your private key and seed words for you.

Wallet name is the
Devotional date

Wallet name
November 13

Derivation path
ot/micah/7/7

Derivation path is the
Scripture passage

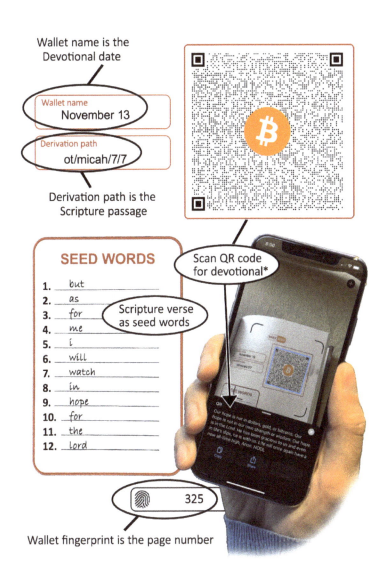

SEED WORDS

1. but
2. as
3. for
4. me
5. i
6. will
7. watch
8. in
9. hope
10. for
11. the
12. Lord

Scan QR code
for devotional*

Scripture verse
as seed words

325

Wallet fingerprint is the page number

*QR Pro** by Crypto Inc (iOS) and **QR & Barcode Scanner** by Gamma Play
(Android) work well.

V

Daily Seed

DAILY SEED

Wallet name
January 1

Derivation path
nt/john/3/16

SEED WORDS

1. for
2. god
3. so
4. loved
5. the
6. world
7. he
8. gave
9. his
10. only
11. begotten
12. son

SEED WORDS

13. that
14. whoever
15. believes
16. in
17. him
18. will
19. not
20. perish
21. but
22. have
23. eternal
24. life

Wallet name
January 2

Derivation path
ot/proverbs/11/1

SEED WORDS

1. the
2. lord
3. detests
4. dishonest
5. scales
6. but
7. accurate
8. weights
9. find
10. favor
11. with
12. him

Wallet name
January 3

Derivation path
ot/proverbs/13/11

SEED WORDS

1. riches
2. obtained
3. by
4. fraud
5. dwindles
6. but
7. wealth
8. obtained
9. by
10. hard
11. work
12. increases

Bitcoin Genesis Block
Raw Hex Version

```
00000000  01 00 00 00 00 00 00 00  00 00 00 00 00 00 00 00   ................
00000010  00 00 00 00 00 00 00 00  00 00 00 00 00 00 00 00   ................
00000020  00 00 00 00 3B A3 ED FD  7A 7B 12 B2 7A C7 2C 3E   ....;£íý·z{.²z.,>
00000030  67 76 8F 61 7F C8 1B C3  88 8A 51 32 3A 9F B8 AA   gv.a.È.Ã.SQ2:Ÿ.ª
00000040  4B 1E 5E 4A 29 AB 5F 49  FF FF 00 1D 1D AC 2B 7C   K.^J).«_Iÿÿ...¬+|
00000050  01 01 00 00 00 01 00 00  00 00 00 00 00 00 00 00   ................
00000060  00 00 00 00 00 00 00 00  00 00 00 00 00 00 00 00   ................
00000070  00 00 00 00 00 00 FF FF  FF FF 4D 04 FF FF 00 1D   ......ÿÿÿÿM.ÿÿ..
00000080  01 04 45 54 68 65 20 54  69 6D 65 73 20 30 33 2F   ..EThe Times 03/
00000090  4A 61 6E 2F 32 30 30 39  20 43 68 61 6E 63 65 6C   Jan/2009 Chancel
000000A0  6C 6F 72 20 6F 6E 20 62  72 69 6E 6B 20 6F 66 20   lor on brink of
000000B0  73 65 63 6F 6E 64 20 62  61 69 6C 6F 75 74 20 66   second bailout f
000000C0  6F 72 20 62 61 6E 6B 73  FF FF FF FF 01 00 F2 05   or banksÿÿÿÿ..ò.
000000D0  2A 01 00 00 00 43 41 04  67 8A FD B0 FE 55 48 27   *....CA.gŠý°þUH'
000000E0  19 67 F1 A6 71 30 B7 10  5C D6 A8 28 E0 39 09 A6   .gñ¦q0·.\Ö¨(à9..¦
000000F0  79 62 E0 EA 1F 61 DE B6  49 F6 BC 3F 4C EF 38 C4   ybàê.aÞ¶Iö¼?Lï8Ä
00000100  F3 55 04 E5 1E C1 12 DE  5C 38 4D F7 BA 0B BD 57   óU.å.Á.Þ\8M÷º.½W
00000110  8A 4C 70 2B 6B F1 1D 5F  AC 00 00 00 00           ŠLp+kñ._¬....
```

"The Times 03/Jan/2009 Chancelor on brink of second bailout for banks"

Wallet name
January 4

Derivation path
nt/luke/17/6

SEED WORDS

1. if
2. you
3. had
4. faith
5. like
6. a
7. mustard
8. seed
9. you
10. could
11. say
12. to

SEED WORDS

13. this
14. tree
15. be
16. uprooted
17. and
18. planted
19. in
20. the
21. sea
22. and
23. it
24. would

DAILY SEED

Wallet name
January 5

Derivation path
ot/proverbs/22/7

SEED WORDS

1. the
2. rich
3. rule
4. over
5. the
6. poor
7. the
8. borrower
9. is
10. slave
11. to
12. lender

DAILY SEED

Wallet name
January 6

Derivation path
nt/galatians/5/1

SEED WORDS

1. it
2. is
3. for
4. freedom
5. that
6. christ
7. has
8. set
9. us
10. free
11. stand
12. firm

Wallet name
January 7

Derivation path
nt/1thess/5/16/18

SEED WORDS

1. rejoice
2. always
3. pray
4. continually
5. and
6. give
7. thanks
8. in
9. all
10. circumstances
11. for
12. this

SEED WORDS

13. is
14. the
15. will
16. of
17. god
18. for
19. you
20. in
21. Christ
22. Jesus
23. our
24. lord

DAILY SEED

Wallet name
January 8

Derivation path
ot/numbers/6/24/26

SEED WORDS

1. the
2. lord
3. bless
4. you
5. keep
6. you
7. make
8. his
9. face
10. shine
11. upon
12. you

SEED WORDS

13. be
14. gracious
15. to
16. you
17. turn
18. his
19. face
20. toward
21. you
22. give
23. you
24. peace

Wallet name
January 9

Derivation path
ot/psalm/85/9

SEED WORDS

1. salvation
2. is
3. near
4. to
5. those
6. who
7. fear
8. him
9. and
10. glory
11. fills
12. the

Passphrase: land

Wallet name
January 10

Derivation path
ot/eccles/4/9

SEED WORDS

1. two
2. are
3. better
4. than
5. one
6. they
7. have
8. a
9. good
10. return
11. on
12. labor

halfin
@halfin

Running bitcoin

7:33 PM - 10 Jan 2009

💬 316   🔁 3.3K   ♡ 8.1K   ✉

Wallet name
January 11

Derivation path
nt/phil/4/6

SEED WORDS

1. be
2. anxious
3. for
4. nothing
5. but
6. with
7. prayer
8. and
9. supplication
10. pray
11. to
12. god

DAILY SEED

Wallet name
January 12

Derivation path
ot/deut/6/6

SEED WORDS

1. talk
2. about
3. my
4. commandments
5. when
6. you
7. sit
8. at
9. home
10. and
11. when
12. you

SEED WORDS

13. walk
14. along
15. the
16. road
17. when
18. you
19. lie
20. down
21. when
22. you
23. get
24. up

DAILY **SEED**

Wallet name
January 13

Derivation path
ot/jeremiah/29/11

SEED WORDS

1. for
2. i
3. know
4. the
5. plans
6. i
7. have
8. for
9. you
10. declares
11. the
12. lord

SEED WORDS

13. plans
14. to
15. prosper
16. you
17. and
18. to
19. give
20. you
21. hope
22. and
23. a
24. future

Wallet name
January 14

Derivation path
ot/proverbs/16/3

SEED WORDS

1. commit
2. to
3. the
4. lord
5. whatever
6. you
7. do
8. and
9. he
10. will
11. establish
12. your

Passphrase: plans

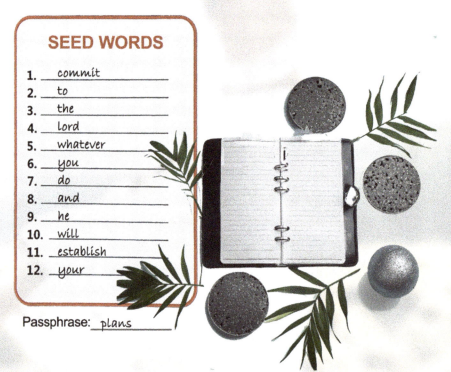

Wallet name
January 15

Derivation path
ot/isaiah/41/10

SEED WORDS

1. do
2. not
3. fear
4. for
5. i
6. am
7. with
8. you
9. do
10. not
11. be
12. dismayed

SEED WORDS

13. for
14. i
15. am
16. your
17. god
18. i
19. will
20. strengthen
21. you
22. and
23. help
24. you

DAILY SEED

Wallet name
January 16

Derivation path
nt/mark/11/24

SEED WORDS

1. whatever
2. you
3. ask
4. for
5. in
6. prayer
7. believe
8. that
9. you
10. have
11. received
12. it

Wallet name
January 17

Derivation path
nt/romans/15/13

SEED WORDS

1. may
2. the
3. god
4. of
5. hope
6. fill
7. you
8. with
9. all
10. joy
11. and
12. peace

SEED WORDS

13. as
14. you
15. trust
16. in
17. him
18. so
19. that
20. you
21. may
22. overflow
23. with
24. hope

DAILY SEED

Wallet name
January 18

Derivation path
nt/colossians/3/23

SEED WORDS

1. whatever
2. you
3. do
4. work
5. at
6. it
7. with
8. all
9. your
10. might
11. as
12. working

SEED WORDS

13. for
14. the
15. lord
16. not
17. human
18. masters
19. you
20. are
21. serving
22. the
23. lord
24. jesus

Wallet name
January 19

Derivation path
ot/deut/31/8

SEED WORDS

1. the
2. lord
3. himself
4. goes
5. before
6. you
7. and
8. will
9. be
10. with
11. you
12. he

SEED WORDS

13. will
14. never
15. leave
16. you
17. or
18. forsake
19. you
20. therefore
21. do
22. not
23. be
24. afraid

Wallet name
January 20

Derivation path
ot/songofsolomon/2/1

SEED WORDS

1. i
2. am
3. the
4. rose
5. of
6. Sharon
7. and
8. the
9. lily
10. of
11. the
12. valley

DAILY SEED

Wallet name
January 21

Derivation path
nt/acts/16/31

SEED WORDS

1. believe
2. in
3. the
4. lord
5. jesus
6. and
7. you
8. and
9. your
10. house
11. will
12. be

Passphrase: saved

DAILY SEED

Wallet name
January 22

Derivation path
ot/proverbs/3/5

SEED WORDS

1. trust
2. in
3. the
4. lord
5. with
6. all
7. your
8. heart
9. and
10. do
11. not
12. lean

SEED WORDS

13. on
14. your
15. own
16. understanding
17. but
18. in
19. all
20. your
21. ways
22. submit
23. to
24. him

DAILY SEED

Wallet name
January 23

Derivation path
nt/john/11/25

SEED WORDS

1. jesus
2. said
3. to
4. her
5. i
6. am
7. the
8. resurrection
9. i
10. am
11. the
12. life

Wallet name
January 24

Derivation path
nt/hebrews/11/1

SEED WORDS

1. faith
2. is
3. confidence
4. in
5. what
6. we
7. hope
8. for
9. assurance
10. in
11. what
12. we

Passphrase: _cannot see_

Wallet name
January 25

Derivation path
nt/ephesians/4/2

SEED WORDS

1. be
2. completely
3. humble
4. and
5. gentle
6. be
7. patient
8. bear
9. with
10. one
11. another
12. in

Passphrase: love

DAILY SEED

Wallet name
January 26

Derivation path
ot/exodus/23/25

SEED WORDS

1. worship
2. the
3. lord
4. your
5. god
6. and
7. his
8. blessing
9. will
10. be
11. on
12. your

SEED WORDS

13. food
14. and
15. your
16. water
17. he
18. will
19. take
20. away
21. sickness
22. from
23. among
24. you

Wallet name
January 27

Derivation path
nt/2corinthians/3/17

SEED WORDS

1. now
2. brothers
3. where
4. the
5. spirit
6. of
7. the
8. lord
9. is
10. there
11. is
12. freedom

Wallet name
January 28

Derivation path
nt/1corinthians/6/9

SEED WORDS

1. do
2. you
3. not
4. know
5. wrongdoers
6. will
7. not
8. inherit
9. the
10. kingdom
11. of
12. god

Wallet name
January 29

Derivation path
nt/john/16/33

SEED WORDS

1. i
2. told
3. you
4. this
5. so
6. you
7. may
8. have
9. peace
10. in
11. me
12. in

SEED WORDS

13. this
14. world
15. you
16. will
17. have
18. trouble
19. take
20. heart
21. i
22. overcame
23. the
24. world

Wallet name
January 30

Derivation path
nt/acts/16/25

SEED WORDS

1. at
2. about
3. midnight
4. paul
5. and
6. silas
7. were
8. praying
9. aloud
10. and
11. singing
12. songs

SEED WORDS

13. of
14. praise
15. to
16. god
17. and
18. the
19. other
20. prisoners
21. were
22. listening
23. to
24. them

Wallet name
January 31

Derivation path
ot/psalm/133/1

SEED WORDS

1. how
2. good
3. and
4. pleasant
5. it
6. is
7. when
8. god's
9. people
10. live
11. in
12. unity

DAILY SEED

Wallet name
February 1

Derivation path
nt/john/1/1-2

SEED WORDS

1. in
2. the
3. beginning
4. was
5. the
6. word
7. and
8. the
9. word
10. was
11. with
12. god

SEED WORDS

13. and
14. the
15. word
16. was
17. god
18. he
19. was
20. with
21. god
22. in
23. the
24. beginning

33

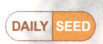

Wallet name

February 2

Derivation path

nt/john/1/3

SEED WORDS

1. through
2. him
3. all
4. things
5. were
6. made
7. and
8. nothing
9. was
10. made
11. without
12. him

BIP-39 Words

abandon ability able about above absent absorb
adapt add addict address adjust admit adult adv
alley allow almost alone alpha already also alter
another answer antenna antique anxiety any a
arrow art artefact artist artwork ask aspect ass
average avocado avoid awake aware away awe
barrel base basic basket battle beach bean bea
bicycle bid bike bind biology bird birth bitter bla
book boost border boring borrow boss bottom
broom brother brown brush bubble buddy budge
cactus cage cake call calm camera camp can
casino castle casual cat catalog catch category
chapter charge chase chat cheap check cheese
claim clap clarify claw clay clean clerk clever cli
coin collect color column combine come comfort
corn correct cost cotton couch country couple c
critic crop cross crouch crowd crucial cruel cru
damage damp dance danger daring dash daugh
deliver demand demise denial dentist deny depar
dial diamond diary dice diesel diet differ digital
dizzy doctor document dog doll dolphin domai
drum dry duck dumb dune during dust dutch d
either elbow elder electric elegant element eleph
enemy energy enforce engage engine enhance
escape essay essence estate eternal ethics evid
exotic expand expect expire explain expose ex
fashion fat fatal father fatigue fault favorite fe
finger finish fire firm first fiscal fish fit fitness f

Wallet name
February 3

Derivation path
nt/john/1/14

SEED WORDS

1. the
2. word
3. became
4. flesh
5. and
6. dwelt
7. among
8. us
9. we
10. have
11. seen
12. his

Passphrase: glory

DAILY SEED

Wallet name
February 4

Derivation path
ot/amos/5/24

SEED WORDS

1. let
2. justice
3. roll
4. down
5. like
6. waters
7. and
8. righteousness
9. like
10. an
11. everflowing
12. stream

Wallet name
February 5

Derivation path
nt/romans/12/2

SEED WORDS

1. do
2. not
3. conform
4. to
5. this
6. world
7. be
8. transformed
9. by
10. renewing
11. of
12. your

Passphrase: _mind_

DAILY SEED

Wallet name
February 6

Derivation path
nt/philippians/4/13

SEED WORDS

1. for
2. i
3. can
4. do
5. all
6. things
7. through
8. him
9. who
10. gives
11. me
12. strength

DAILY SEED

Wallet name
February 7

Derivation path
nt/john/14/6

SEED WORDS

1. jesus
2. answered
3. and
4. said
5. to
6. them
7. i
8. am
9. the
10. way
11. the
12. truth

SEED WORDS

13. and
14. the
15. life
16. no
17. one
18. comes
19. to
20. the
21. father
22. except
23. through
24. me

Wallet name
February 8

Derivation path
ot/proverbs/1/7

SEED WORDS

1. the
2. fear
3. of
4. the
5. lord
6. is
7. the
8. beginning
9. of
10. knowledge
11. and
12. wisdom

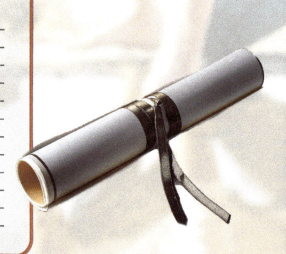

DAILY SEED

Wallet name
February 9

Derivation path
ot/psalm/104/33

SEED WORDS

1. i
2. will
3. sing
4. praise
5. to
6. the
7. lord
8. as
9. long
10. as
11. i
12. live

DAILY SEED

Wallet name
February 10

Derivation path
ot/psalm/100/1

SEED WORDS

1. make
2. a
3. joyful
4. noise
5. to
6. the
7. lord
8. all
9. the
10. earth
11. give
12. thanks

42

DAILY SEED

Wallet name
February 11

Derivation path
ot/psalm/103/19

SEED WORDS

1. the
2. lord
3. has
4. established
5. his
6. throne
7. and
8. his
9. kingdom
10. rules
11. over
12. all

DAILY SEED

Wallet name
February 12

Derivation path
ot/isaiah/41/13

SEED WORDS

1. for
2. i
3. am
4. the
5. lord
6. god
7. who
8. takes
9. hold
10. of
11. your
12. right

SEED WORDS

13. hand
14. and
15. says
16. to
17. you
18. do
19. not
20. fear
21. i
22. will
23. help
24. you

44

Wallet name
February 13

Derivation path
ot/proverbs/11/25

SEED WORDS

1. a
2. generous
3. person
4. will
5. prosper
6. and
7. whoever
8. refreshes
9. others
10. will
11. be
12. refreshed

SEED WORDS

1. there
2. is
3. no
4. greater
5. love
6. than
7. to
8. lay
9. down
10. your
11. life
12. for

Passphrase: another

Wallet name
February 15

Derivation path
nt/1timothy/6/10

SEED WORDS

1. for
2. the
3. love
4. of
5. money
6. is
7. the
8. root
9. of
10. all
11. kinds
12. of

SEED WORDS

13. evil
14. and
15. through
16. this
17. craving
18. some
19. have
20. wandered
21. away
22. from
23. the
24. faith

DAILY SEED

Wallet name
February 16

Derivation path
nt/1thess/5/11

SEED WORDS

1. encourage
2. one
3. another
4. and
5. build
6. each
7. other
8. up
9. just
10. as
11. you
12. are

Passphrase: doing

DAILY SEED

Wallet name
February 17

Derivation path
nt/1corinth/6/20

SEED WORDS

1. for
2. you
3. are
4. not
5. your
6. own
7. you
8. were
9. bought
10. with
11. a
12. price

49

Wallet name
February 18

Derivation path
ot/joshua/1/9

SEED WORDS

1. have
2. i
3. not
4. commanded
5. you
6. be
7. strong
8. and
9. courageous
10. do
11. not
12. fear

50

Wallet name
February 19

Derivation path
ot/1chronicles/16/34

SEED WORDS

1. give
2. thanks
3. to
4. the
5. lord
6. he
7. is
8. good
9. his
10. love
11. endures
12. forever

DAILY SEED

Wallet name
February 20

Derivation path
ot/proverbs/4/23

SEED WORDS

1. above
2. all
3. guard
4. your
5. heart
6. for
7. everything
8. you
9. do
10. flows
11. from
12. it

DAILY SEED

Wallet name
February 21

Derivation path
ot/proverbs/27/19

SEED WORDS

1. as
2. water
3. reflects
4. the
5. face
6. the
7. way
8. you
9. live
10. reflects
11. the
12. heart

53

DAILY SEED

Wallet name
February 22

Derivation path
nt/james/5/16

SEED WORDS

1. confess
2. your
3. sins
4. to
5. one
6. another
7. and
8. pray
9. for
10. each
11. other
12. that

SEED WORDS

13. you
14. may
15. be
16. healed
17. the
18. prayer
19. of
20. a
21. righteous
22. person
23. is
24. powerful

Wallet name
February 23

Derivation path
nt/1corinthians/15/57

SEED WORDS

1. thanks
2. be
3. to
4. god
5. who
6. gves
7. us
8. the
9. victory
10. in
11. jesus
12. christ

DAILY SEED

Wallet name
February 24

Derivation path
ot/isaiah/49/15-16

SEED WORDS

1. can
2. a
3. mother
4. forget
5. the
6. baby
7. at
8. her
9. breast
10. i
11. will
12. not

SEED WORDS

13. forget
14. you
15. i
16. have
17. engraved
18. you
19. on
20. the
21. palms
22. of
23. my
24. hands

Wallet name
February 25

Derivation path
nt/philippians/2/3

SEED WORDS

1. do
2. nothing
3. out
4. of
5. selfish
6. ambition
7. in
8. humility
9. value
10. others
11. above
12. yourselves

Wallet name
February 26

Derivation path
nt/galatians/6/9

SEED WORDS

1. let
2. us
3. not
4. become
5. weary
6. in
7. doing
8. good
9. for
10. at
11. the
12. proper

SEED WORDS

13. time
14. we
15. will
16. reap
17. a
18. harvest
19. if
20. we
21. do
22. not
23. give
24. up

Wallet name
February 27

Derivation path
nt/2timothy/1/7-8

SEED WORDS

1. for
2. god
3. has
4. not
5. given
6. us
7. a
8. spirit
9. of
10. fear
11. but
12. of

SEED WORDS

13. power
14. and
15. love
16. and
17. a
18. sound
19. mind
20. so
21. do
22. not
23. be
24. ashamed

Wallet name
February 28

Derivation path
nt/mark/10/27

SEED WORDS

1. with
2. man
3. this
4. is
5. impossible
6. but
7. with
8. god
9. all
10. things
11. are
12. possible

Wallet name
February 29

Derivation path
ot/jeremiah/29/13

SEED WORDS

1. you
2. will
3. find
4. me
5. when
6. you
7. seek
8. me
9. with
10. your
11. whole
12. heart

Wallet name
March 1

Derivation path
ot/proverbs/11/9

SEED WORDS

1. with
2. their
3. mouths
4. the
5. godless
6. destroy
7. their
8. neighbors
9. through
10. knowledge
11. the
12. righteous

Passphrase: escape

DAILY SEED

Wallet name
March 2

Derivation path
ot/micah/6/8

SEED WORDS

1. he
2. has
3. shown
4. you
5. what
6. is
7. good
8. and
9. what
10. the
11. Lord
12. requires

SEED WORDS

13. of
14. you
15. do
16. justly
17. love
18. mercy
19. and
20. walk
21. humbly
22. with
23. your
24. god

DAILY SEED

Wallet name
March 3

Derivation path
ot/exodus/22/11

SEED WORDS

1. for
2. in
3. six
4. days
5. the
6. lord
7. made
8. the
9. heavens
10. and
11. the
12. earth

Wallet name
March 4

Derivation path
ot/habakkuk/1/3

SEED WORDS

1. why
2. do
3. you
4. show
5. me
6. injustice
7. and
8. cause
9. me
10. to
11. see
12. trouble

SEED WORDS

13. for
14. plundering
15. and
16. violence
17. are
18. before
19. me
20. and
21. strife
22. and
23. conflict
24. abound

Wallet name
March 5

Derivation path
nt/colossians/3/5-6

SEED WORDS

1. put
2. to
3. death
4. therefore
5. your
6. earthly
7. nature
8. sexual
9. immorality
10. impurity
11. lust
12. evil

SEED WORDS

13. desires
14. and
15. greed
16. because
17. of
18. these
19. the
20. wrath
21. of
22. god
23. is
24. coming

DAILY SEED

Wallet name
March 6

Derivation path
nt/3john/1/11

SEED WORDS

1. do
2. not
3. imitate
4. what
5. is
6. evil
7. but
8. what
9. is
10. good
11. anyone
12. doing

SEED WORDS

13. good
14. is
15. from
16. god
17. but
18. anyone
19. doing
20. evil
21. is
22. not
23. from
24. god

68

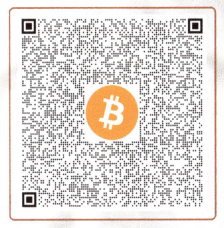

DAILY SEED

Wallet name
March 7

Derivation path
ot/proverbs/23/10-11

SEED WORDS

1. do
2. not
3. move
4. an
5. ancient
6. boundary
7. stone
8. or
9. encroach
10. on
11. the
12. fields

SEED WORDS

13. of
14. the
15. fartherless
16. their
17. defender
18. is
19. strong
20. he
21. will
22. take
23. their
24. case

DAILY SEED

Wallet name
March 8

Derivation path
ot/proverbs/2/2

SEED WORDS

1. my
2. son
3. turn
4. your
5. ear
6. to
7. wisdom
8. and
9. your
10. heart
11. to
12. understanding

Wallet name
March 9

Derivation path
ot/numbers/25//3

SEED WORDS

1. they
2. yoked
3. themselves
4. to
5. baal
6. and
7. the
8. lord's
9. anger
10. burned
11. against
12. them

DAILY SEED

Wallet name
March 10

Derivation path
nt/luke/12/7

SEED WORDS

1. god
2. knows
3. the
4. number
5. of
6. hairs
7. on
8. your
9. head
10. be
11. not
12. afraid

DAILY SEED

Wallet name
March 11

Derivation path
nt/philemon/1/4

SEED WORDS

1. i
2. always
3. thank
4. my
5. god
6. as
7. i
8. remember
9. you
10. in
11. my
12. prayers

DAILY SEED

Wallet name
March 12

Derivation path
nt/hebrews/13/8

SEED WORDS

1. our
2. lord
3. jesus
4. christ
5. is
6. the
7. same
8. yesterday
9. and
10. today
11. and
12. forever

Wallet name
March 13

Derivation path
nt/acts3/6

SEED WORDS

1. silver
2. and
3. gold
4. i
5. do
6. not
7. have
8. but
9. what
10. i
11. do
12. have

SEED WORDS

13. i
14. give
15. to
16. you
17. in
18. the
19. name
20. of
21. jesus
22. stand
23. and
24. walk

Wallet name
March 14

Derivation path
nt/2timothy/3/1

SEED WORDS

1. but
2. know
3. this
4. that
5. in
6. the
7. last
8. days
9. perilous
10. times
11. will
12. come

Wallet name
March 15

Derivation path
nt/john/1/5

SEED WORDS

1. the
2. light
3. shines
4. in
5. the
6. darkness
7. and
8. the
9. darkness
10. cannot
11. overcome
12. it

Wallet name
March 16

Derivation path
nt/john/13/5

SEED WORDS

1. he
2. poured
3. water
4. into
5. a
6. basin
7. and
8. began
9. to
10. wash
11. their
12. feet

DAILY SEED

Wallet name
March 17

Derivation path
nt/galatians/6/8

SEED WORDS

1. for
2. whoever
3. sows
4. to
5. please
6. their
7. flesh
8. will
9. reap
10. destruction
11. but
12. whoever

SEED WORDS

13. sows
14. to
15. please
16. the
17. spirit
18. will
19. from
20. the
21. spirit
22. reap
23. eternal
24. life

Wallet name
March 18

Derivation path
nt/2thess/3/3

SEED WORDS

1. the
2. lord
3. will
4. establish
5. you
6. and
7. guard
8. you
9. against
10. the
11. evil
12. one

DAILY SEED

Wallet name
March 19

Derivation path
nt/1peter/3/15

SEED WORDS

1. always
2. be
3. ready
4. to
5. give
6. an
7. answer
8. for
9. the
10. hope
11. you
12. have

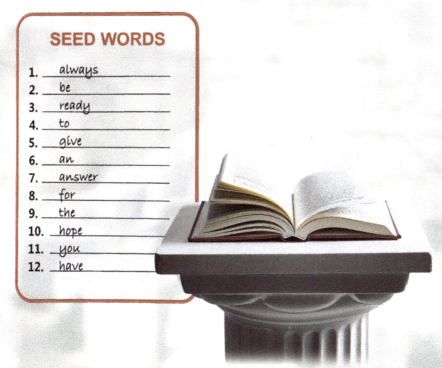

Wallet name
March 20

Derivation path
ot/ecclesiastes/5/10

SEED WORDS

1. whoever
2. loves
3. money
4. never
5. has
6. enough
7. whoever
8. loves
9. wealth
10. is
11. never
12. satisfied

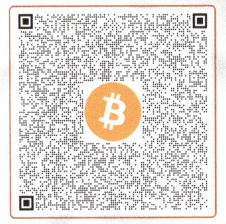

DAILY SEED

Wallet name
March 21

Derivation path
nt/revelation/21/21

SEED WORDS

1. the
2. great
3. street
4. of
5. the
6. city
7. was
8. pure
9. gold
10. like
11. transparent
12. glass

DAILY SEED

Wallet name
March 22

Derivation path
ot/psalm/20/7-8

SEED WORDS

1. some
2. trust
3. in
4. chariots
5. others
6. in
7. horses
8. but
9. we
10. trust
11. in
12. the

SEED WORDS

13. name
14. of
15. the
16. lord
17. our
18. god
19. they
20. will
21. fall
22. we
23. will
24. rise

Wallet name
March 23

Derivation path
ot/psalm/32/1

SEED WORDS

1. blessed
2. is
3. the
4. one
5. whose
6. transgression
7. is
8. forgiven
9. whose
10. sin
11. is
12. covered

Wallet name
March 24

Derivation path
ot/psalm/55/11

SEED WORDS

1. ruin
2. is
3. everywhere
4. oppression
5. and
6. fraud
7. do
8. not
9. depart
10. from
11. the
12. marketplace

DAILY SEED

Wallet name
March 25

Derivation path
nt/revelation/1/18

SEED WORDS

1. i
2. am
3. the
4. living
5. one
6. i
7. was
8. dead
9. and
10. behold
11. now
12. i

SEED WORDS

13. am
14. alive
15. forever
16. and
17. i
18. hold
19. the
20. keys
21. of
22. death
23. and
24. hades

Wallet name
March 26

Derivation path
nt/1corinthians/8/2

SEED WORDS

1. if
2. anyone
3. thinks
4. he
5. knows
6. something
7. he
8. knows
9. nothing
10. as
11. he
12. ought

DAILY SEED

Wallet name
March 27

Derivation path
nt/hebrews/13/1

SEED WORDS

1. keep
2. on
3. loving
4. one
5. another
6. as
7. brothers
8. and
9. sisters
10. in
11. christ
12. jesus

Wallet name
March 28

Derivation path
nt/romans/13/8

SEED WORDS

1. let
2. no
3. debt
4. remain
5. outstanding
6. except
7. the
8. continuing
9. debt
10. to
11. love
12. one

Passphrase: another

90

Wallet name
March 29

Derivation path
nt/philippians/3/7

SEED WORDS

1. but
2. what
3. was
4. gain
5. to
6. me
7. i
8. count
9. as
10. loss
11. for
12. christ

DAILY SEED

Wallet name

March 30

Derivation path

ot/daniel/12/3

SEED WORDS

1. those
2. who
3. are
4. wise
5. will
6. shine
7. like
8. the
9. brightness
10. of
11. heaven
12. and

SEED WORDS

13. those
14. who
15. lead
16. many
17. to
18. righteousness
19. like
20. stars
21. for
22. ever
23. and
24. ever

DAILY SEED

Wallet name
March 31

Derivation path
ot/proverbs/15/6

SEED WORDS

1. there
2. is
3. much
4. treasure
5. found
6. in
7. the
8. house
9. of
10. a
11. righteous
12. person

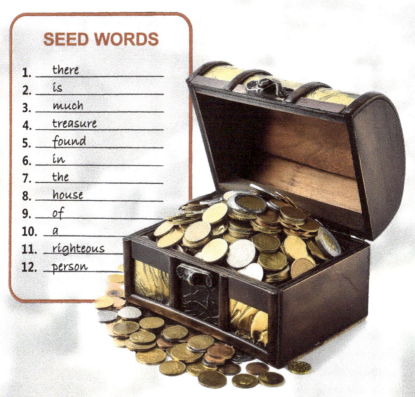

Wallet name
April 1

Derivation path
ot/psalm53/1

SEED WORDS

1. the
2. fool
3. says
4. to
5. himself
6. there
7. is
8. no
9. god
10. he
11. is
12. corrupt

95

Wallet name
April 2

Derivation path
nt/colossians/2/9-10

SEED WORDS

1. in
2. christ
3. dwells
4. all
5. the
6. fullness
7. of
8. the
9. deity
10. in
11. bodily
12. form

SEED WORDS

13. and
14. you
15. are
16. complete
17. in
18. him
19. who
20. is
21. the
22. head
23. over
24. all

Wallet name
April 3

Derivation path
nt/colossians/2/4

SEED WORDS

1. i
2. tell
3. you
4. these
5. things
6. so
7. that
8. you
9. will
10. not
11. be
12. deceived

DAILY SEED

Wallet name
April 4

Derivation path
ot/psalm/37/1-2

SEED WORDS

1. do
2. not
3. fret
4. because
5. of
6. those
7. who
8. do
9. evil
10. or
11. be
12. envious

SEED WORDS

13. of
14. those
15. who
16. do
17. wrong
18. like
19. grass
20. they
21. will
22. soon
23. wither
24. away

DAILY SEED

Wallet name
April 5

Derivation path
ot/joel/3/5

SEED WORDS

1. for
2. you
3. took
4. my
5. silver
6. and
7. gold
8. and
9. carried
10. off
11. my
12. treasure

6102

DAILY SEED

Wallet name
April 6

Derivation path
ot/genesis/3/15

SEED WORDS

1. i
2. will
3. put
4. emnity
5. between
6. you
7. and
8. the
9. woman
10. and
11. your
12. offspring

SEED WORDS

13. and
14. hers
15. he
16. will
17. crush
18. your
19. head
20. you
21. will
22. strike
23. his
24. heel

Wallet name
April 7

Derivation path
ot/job/42/2

SEED WORDS

1. you
2. can
3. do
4. all
5. things
6. no
7. purpose
8. of
9. yours
10. can
11. be
12. thwarted

DAILY SEED

Wallet name
April 8

Derivation path
nt/1john/1/9-10

SEED WORDS

1. if
2. we
3. claim
4. to
5. be
6. without
7. sin
8. we
9. deceive
10. ourselves
11. but
12. if

SEED WORDS

13. we
14. confess
15. our
16. sins
17. he
18. is
19. faithful
20. and
21. just
22. to
23. forgive
24. us

DAILY SEED

Wallet name
April 9

Derivation path
nt/jude/1/1-2

SEED WORDS

1. to
2. those
3. who
4. are
5. called
6. who
7. are
8. loved
9. in
10. god
11. the
12. father

SEED WORDS

13. and
14. kept
15. for
16. jesus
17. christ
18. mercy
19. peace
20. and
21. love
22. be
23. yours
24. abundantly

Wallet name
April 10

Derivation path
nt/james/5/4

SEED WORDS

1. the
2. wages
3. you
4. failed
5. to
6. pay
7. the
8. workers
9. who
10. mowed
11. your
12. fields

SEED WORDS

13. are
14. crying
15. out
16. against
17. you
18. their
19. cries
20. have
21. been
22. heard
23. by
24. god

DAILY SEED

Wallet name
April 11

Derivation path
nt/james/5/7

SEED WORDS

1. be
2. patient
3. for
4. the
5. lord's
6. coming
7. see
8. how
9. the
10. farmer
11. waits
12. for

SEED WORDS

13. the
14. land
15. to
16. yield
17. its
18. valuable
19. crop
20. patiently
21. waiting
22. for
23. the
24. rain

Wallet name
April 12

Derivation path
nt/matthew/7/8

SEED WORDS

1. for
2. everyone
3. who
4. asks
5. receives
6. and
7. the
8. one
9. who
10. seeks
11. will
12. find

DAILY SEED

Wallet name
April 13

Derivation path
nt/philippians/4/4

SEED WORDS

1. rejoice
2. in
3. the
4. lord
5. always
6. and
7. i
8. will
9. say
10. it
11. again
12. rejoice

Wallet name
April 14

Derivation path
ot/daniel/6/4

SEED WORDS

1. they
2. tried
3. to
4. find
5. grounds
6. for
7. charges
8. against
9. daniel
10. but
11. could
12. find

Passphrase: none

Wallet name
April 15

Derivation path
nt/mark/12/17

SEED WORDS

1. render
2. unto
3. caesar
4. what
5. is
6. caesar's
7. and
8. to
9. god
10. what
11. is
12. god's

← **Post**

Nayib Bukele ✔ 🫡
@nayibbukele   ···

We've decided to transfer a big chunk of our #Bitcoin ₿ to a cold wallet, and store that cold wallet in a physical vault within our national territory.

You can call it our first #Bitcoin ₿ piggy bank 🇸🇻

It's not much, but it's honest work 😂

Address 82vEsVJWu3emuJGMT2qSjAQVZZewwqzo ⬧

Total received	5,689.68509200	
Total sent	0.00000000	
Balance	5,689.68509200	
	$205,607,666	

10:55 am · 15/3/2024 From Earth · **446K** Views

1.7K Reposts **430** Quotes

Wallet name
April 16

Derivation path
nt/john/9/27

SEED WORDS

1. he
2. answered
3. i
4. have
5. told
6. you
7. already
8. and
9. you
10. did
11. not
12. listen

DAILY SEED

Wallet name
April 17

Derivation path
nt/acts/1/3

SEED WORDS

1. after
2. his
3. suffering
4. he
5. presented
6. himself
7. to
8. them
9. giving
10. many
11. convincing
12. proofs

SEED WORDS

13. he
14. was
15. alive
16. he
17. appeared
18. forty
19. days
20. and
21. spoke
22. about
23. his
24. kingdom

DAILY SEED

Wallet name
April 18

Derivation path
nt/galatians/6/7

SEED WORDS

1. be
2. not
3. deceived
4. god
5. cannot
6. be
7. mocked
8. man
9. reaps
10. what
11. he
12. sows

Wallet name
April 19

Derivation path
nt/2corinthians/3/18

SEED WORDS

1. we
2. are
3. being
4. transformed
5. into
6. his
7. image
8. going
9. from
10. glory
11. to
12. glory

DAILY SEED

Wallet name
April 20

Derivation path
ot/1kings/2/2-3

SEED WORDS

1. be
2. strong
3. act
4. like
5. a
6. man
7. and
8. do
9. all
10. the
11. Lord
12. requries

DAILY SEED

Wallet name
April 21

Derivation path
nt/2peter/1/3

SEED WORDS

1. his
2. divine
3. power
4. has
5. given
6. us
7. everything
8. we
9. need
10. for
11. godly
12. living

Wallet name
April 22

Derivation path
nt/titus/3/3-4

SEED WORDS

1. once
2. we
3. were
4. also
5. foolish
6. disobedient
7. and
8. filled
9. with
10. malice
11. and
12. envy

SEED WORDS

13. but
14. then
15. the
16. kndness
17. of
18. god
19. our
20. savior
21. appeared
22. and
23. saved
24. us

DAILY SEED

Wallet name
April 23

Derivation path
nt/1corinthians/3/5

SEED WORDS

1. who
2. after
3. all
4. is
5. paul
6. and
7. who
8. is
9. apollos
10. but
11. merely
12. servants

From: Satoshi Nakamoto <satoshin@gmx.com>
Date: Sat, Apr 23, 2011 at 3:40 PM
To: Mike Hearn <mike@plan99.net>

   I had a few other things on my mind (as always). One is, are you planning on rejoining the community at some point (eg for
code reviews), or is your plan to permanently step back from the limelight?

I've moved on to other things. It's in good hands with Gavin and everyone.

Wallet name
April 24

Derivation path
nt/ephesians/4/3

SEED WORDS

1. make
2. every
3. effort
4. to
5. keep
6. unity
7. of
8. spirit
9. through
10. bond
11. of
12. peace

Wallet name
April 25

Derivation path
nt/1thessalonians/5/3

SEED WORDS

1. while
2. people
3. are
4. saying
5. peace
6. and
7. safety
8. destruction
9. will
10. come
11. on
12. them

SEED WORDS

13. suddenly
14. as
15. labor
16. pains
17. on
18. a
19. pregnant
20. woman
21. they
22. will
23. not
24. escape

Wallet name
April 26

Derivation path
nt/2thessalonians/3/2

SEED WORDS

1. and
2. pray
3. that
4. we
5. may
6. be
7. delivered
8. from
9. wicked
10. and
11. evil
12. people

Wallet name
April 27

Derivation path
nt/romans/7/24-25

SEED WORDS

1. what
2. a
3. wretched
4. man
5. i
6. am
7. who
8. will
9. deliver
10. me
11. from
12. this

SEED WORDS

13. body
14. of
15. death
16. thanks
17. be
18. to
19. god
20. through
21. our
22. lord
23. jesus
24. christ

Wallet name
April 28

Derivation path
nt/matthew/6/2

SEED WORDS

1. so
2. when
3. you
4. give
5. to
6. the
7. needy
8. do
9. not
10. announce
11. it
12. with

Passphrase: trumpets

Wallet name
April 29

Derivation path
ot/isaiah/52/7

SEED WORDS

1. how
2. beautiful
3. on
4. the
5. mountain
6. are
7. the
8. feet
9. of
10. those
11. bringing
12. good

Passphrase: news

123

DAILY SEED

Wallet name
April 30

Derivation path
ot/isaiah/55/9

SEED WORDS

1. as
2. the
3. heavens
4. are
5. higher
6. than
7. the
8. earth
9. so
10. my
11. ways
12. are

SEED WORDS

13. higher
14. than
15. your
16. ways
17. and
18. my
19. thoughts
20. are
21. higher
22. than
23. your
24. thoughts

DAILY SEED

Wallet name

May 1

Derivation path

ot/2chronicles/30/12

SEED WORDS

1. the
2. hand
3. of
4. god
5. was
6. on
7. the
8. people
9. to
10. give
11. them
12. unity

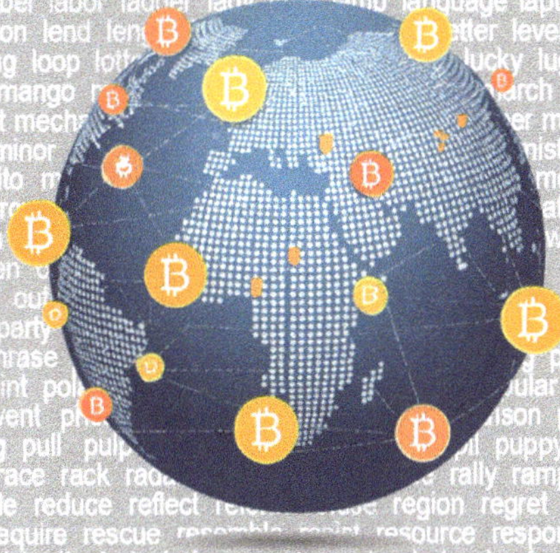

125

Wallet name
May 2

Derivation path
nt/john/10/28

SEED WORDS

1. jesus
2. said
3. i
4. give
5. them
6. eternal
7. life
8. and
9. they
10. shall
11. never
12. perish

126

DAILY SEED

Wallet name
May 3

Derivation path
ot/psalm/86/5

SEED WORDS

1. lord
2. you
3. are
4. forgiving
5. and
6. good
7. abounding
8. in
9. mercy
10. to
11. all
12. who

Passphrase: ask

127

Wallet name

May 4

Derivation path

ot/proverbs/18/16

SEED WORDS

1. see
2. a
3. gift
4. ushers
5. the
6. giver
7. into
8. the
9. presence
10. of
11. great
12. men

Wallet name

May 5

Derivation path

ot/psalm/23/1-2

SEED WORDS

1. the
2. lord
3. is
4. my
5. shepherd
6. i
7. have
8. no
9. wants
10. he
11. makes
12. me

SEED WORDS

13. lie
14. down
15. in
16. green
17. pastures
18. and
19. he
20. leads
21. me
22. beside
23. quiet
24. waters

129

Wallet name

May 6

Derivation path

nt/matthew/25/15

SEED WORDS

1. to
2. one
3. he
4. gave
5. five
6. coins
7. to
8. another
9. he
10. gave
11. two
12. coins

SEED WORDS

13. and
14. to
15. another
16. he
17. gave
18. one
19. coin
20. each
21. according
22. to
23. his
24. abilities

130

DAILY SEED

Wallet name
May 7

Derivation path
nt/romans/12/4

SEED WORDS

1. just
2. as
3. we
4. have
5. many
6. parts
7. to
8. the
9. human
10. body
11. and
12. each

SEED WORDS

13. part
14. has
15. its
16. own
17. function
18. so
19. we
20. are
21. one
22. body
23. in
24. christ

131

Wallet name

May 8

Derivation path

ot/psalm/52/9

SEED WORDS

1. for
2. what
3. you
4. have
5. done
6. i
7. will
8. always
9. praise
10. you
11. in
12. the

SEED WORDS

13. presence
14. of
15. your
16. faithful
17. people
18. and
19. i
20. will
21. hope
22. in
23. your
24. name

Wallet name

May 9

Derivation path

nt/2peter/3/8

SEED WORDS

1. with
2. the
3. lord
4. a
5. day
6. is
7. like
8. a
9. thousand
10. years
11. and
12. a

SEED WORDS

13. thousand
14. years
15. is
16. like
17. a
18. day
19. he
20. is
21. not
22. slow
23. keeping
24. promises

133

Wallet name

May 10

Derivation path

nt/titus/2/11

SEED WORDS

1. for
2. the
3. grace
4. of
5. god
6. has
7. appeared
8. that
9. offers
10. salvation
11. to
12. all

134

DAILY SEED

Wallet name
May 11

Derivation path
ot/psalm/90/12

SEED WORDS

1. teach
2. us
3. to
4. number
5. our
6. days
7. so
8. that
9. we
10. may
11. gain
12. wisdom

IV

135

Wallet name

May 12

Derivation path

ot/isaiah/26/3

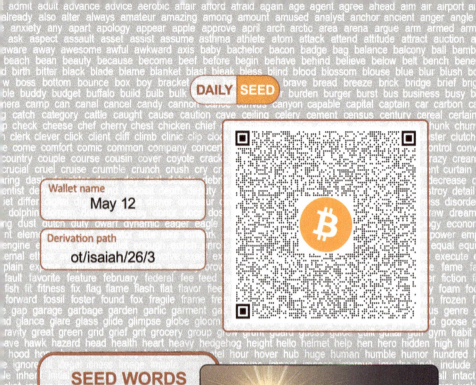

SEED WORDS

1. you
2. will
3. keep
4. in
5. perfect
6. peace
7. him
8. whose
9. mind
10. is
11. stayed
12. on

Passphrase: you

136

Wallet name

May 13

Derivation path

nt/matthew/7/21

SEED WORDS

1. not
2. everyone
3. who
4. says
5. to
6. me
7. lord
8. lord
9. will
10. enter
11. the
12. kingdom

SEED WORDS

13. of
14. heaven
15. but
16. only
17. those
18. who
19. do
20. the
21. will
22. of
23. my
24. father

137

DAILY SEED

Wallet name
May 14

Derivation path
nt/matthew/15/8

SEED WORDS

1. they
2. honor
3. me
4. with
5. their
6. lips
7. but
8. their
9. hearts
10. are
11. far
12. from

Passphrase: me

138

DAILY SEED

Wallet name
May 15

Derivation path
nt/matthew/16/16

SEED WORDS

1. peter
2. answered
3. you
4. are
5. the
6. messiah
7. the
8. son
9. of
10. the
11. living
12. god

139

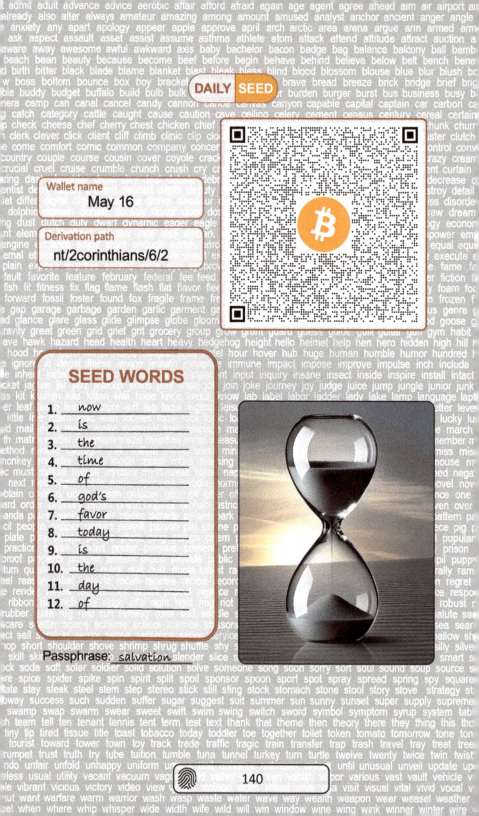

DAILY SEED

Wallet name
May 16

Derivation path
nt/2corinthians/6/2

SEED WORDS

1. now
2. is
3. the
4. time
5. of
6. god's
7. favor
8. today
9. is
10. the
11. day
12. of

Passphrase: salvation

140

Wallet name

May 17

Derivation path

nt/acts/26/8

SEED WORDS

1. why
2. should
3. it
4. be
5. incredible
6. to
7. you
8. that
9. god
10. raises
11. the
12. dead

141

Wallet name

May 18

Derivation path

nt/galatians/5/6

SEED WORDS

1. for
2. in
3. christ
4. jesus
5. neither
6. circumcision
7. nor
8. uncircumcision
9. has
10. any
11. value
12. at

SEED WORDS

13. all
14. the
15. only
16. thing
17. that
18. matters
19. is
20. faith
21. expressing
22. itself
23. through
24. love

142

DAILY SEED

Wallet name
May 19

Derivation path
nt/2corinthians/12/9

SEED WORDS

1. my
2. grace
3. is
4. sufficient
5. for
6. you
7. my
8. power
9. is
10. perfected
11. in
12. your

Passphrase: weakness

143

DAILY SEED

Wallet name
May 20

Derivation path
ot/1kings/3/9

SEED WORDS

1. give
2. your
3. servant
4. a
5. discerning
6. heart
7. to
8. distinguish
9. between
10. right
11. and
12. wrong

144

Wallet name

May 21

Derivation path

nt/2peter/3/4

SEED WORDS

1. they
2. will
3. say
4. where
5. is
6. this
7. 'coming'
8. he
9. promised
10. for
11. ever
12. since

SEED WORDS

13. our
14. ancestors
15. died
16. everything
17. goes
18. on
19. as
20. it
21. has
22. since
23. the
24. beginning

145

Wallet name

May 22

Derivation path

nt/acts/20/28

SEED WORDS

1. shepherd
2. the
3. church
4. of
5. god
6. which
7. he
8. bought
9. with
10. his
11. own
12. blood

146

DAILY SEED

Wallet name
May 23

Derivation path
nt/1corinthians/6/14

SEED WORDS

1. god
2. raised
3. the
4. lord
5. from
6. the
7. dead
8. he
9. wil
10. raise
11. us
12. also

147

Wallet name

May 24

Derivation path

nt/james/1/2

SEED WORDS

1. brothers
2. consider
3. it
4. pure
5. joy
6. whenever
7. you
8. face
9. trials
10. of
11. many
12. kinds

148

Wallet name

May 25

Derivation path

nt/1thessalonians/5/4

SEED WORDS

1. you
2. brothers
3. and
4. sisters
5. are
6. not
7. in
8. the
9. dark
10. so
11. that
12. this

SEED WORDS

13. day
14. should
15. catch
16. you
17. by
18. surprise
19. like
20. a
21. thief
22. in
23. the
24. night

149

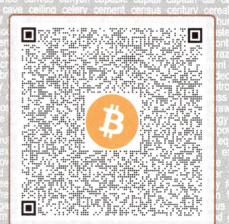

DAILY SEED

Wallet name
May 26

Derivation path
nt/2thessalonians/3/5

SEED WORDS

1. may
2. the
3. lord
4. direct
5. your
6. hearts
7. into
8. god's
9. love
10. and
11. christ's
12. perserverance

150

Wallet name

May 27

Derivation path

ot/psalm/34/22

SEED WORDS

1. not
2. one
3. of
4. those
5. who
6. take
7. refuge
8. in
9. him
10. will
11. be
12. condemned

Wallet name

May 28

Derivation path

nt/luke/7/20

SEED WORDS

1. are
2. you
3. the
4. one
5. to
6. come
7. or
8. should
9. we
10. look
11. for
12. another

152

Wallet name

May 29

Derivation path

ot/proverbs/18/22

SEED WORDS

1. he
2. who
3. finds
4. a
5. wife
6. finds
7. a
8. good
9. thing
10. from
11. the
12. Lord

153

Wallet name

May 30

Derivation path

ot/psalm/118/6

SEED WORDS

1. i
2. will
3. not
4. be
5. afraid
6. what
7. can
8. mere
9. mortals
10. do
11. to
12. me

154

DAILY SEED

Wallet name
May 31

Derivation path
ot/isaiah/1/18

SEED WORDS

1. come
2. now
3. and
4. let
5. us
6. reason
7. together
8. says
9. the
10. lord
11. though
12. your

SEED WORDS

13. sins
14. are
15. dark
16. as
17. scarlet
18. they
19. shall
20. be
21. made
22. white
23. as
24. snow

155

admit adult advance advice aerobic affair afford afraid again age agent agree ahead aim air airport ai
already also alter always amateur amazing among amount amused analyst anchor ancient anger angle
anxiety any apart apology appear apple approve april arch arctic area arena argue arm armed arm
ask aspect assault asset assist assume asthma athlete atom attack attend attitude attract auction a
aware away awesome awful awkward axis baby bachelor bacon badge bag balance balcony ball bamb
beach bean beauty because become beef before begin behave behind believe below belt bench bene
birth bitter black blade blame blanket blast bleak bless blind blood blossom blouse blue blur blush bo
w boss bottom bounce box boy bracket brain brand brass brave bread breeze brick bridge brief brig
ble buddy budget buffalo build bulb bulk bullet bundle bunker burden burger burst bus business busy b
era camp can canal cancel candy cannon canoe canvas canyon capable capital captain car carbon ca
g catch category cattle caught cause caution cave ceiling celery cement census century cereal certain
p check cheese chef cherry chest chicken chief child chimney choice choose chronic chuckle chunk churr
1 clerk clever click client cliff climb clinic clip clock clog close cloth cloud clown club clump cluster clutch
e come comfort comic common company concert conduct confirm congress connect consider control conv
country couple course cousin cover coyote crack cradle craft cram crane crash crater crawl crazy crean
crucial cruel cruise crumble crunch crush cry crystal cube culture cup cupboard curious current curtain
ring dash daughter dawn day deal debate debris decade december decide decline decorate decrease c
entist deny depart depend deposit depth deputy derive describe desert design desk despair destroy detail
iet differ digital dignity dilemma dinner dinosaur direct dirt disagree discover disease dish dismiss disorde
dolphin domain donate donkey donor door dose double dove draft dragon drama drastic draw dream
ng dust dutch duty dwarf dynamic eager eagle early earn earth easily east easy echo ecology econor
nt element elephant elevator elite else embark embody embrace emerge emotion employ empower em
engine enhance enjoy enlist enough enrich enroll ensure enter entire entry envelope episode equal equi
emal ethics evidence evil evoke evolve exact example excess exchange excite exclude excuse execute e
plain expose express extend extra eye eyebrow fabric face faculty fade faint faith fall false fame fa
fault favorite feature february federal fee feed feel female fence festival fetch fever few fiber fiction f
fish fit fitness fix flag flame flash flat flavor flee flight flip float flock floor flower fluid flush fly foam foc
forward fossil foster found fox fragile frame frequent fresh friend fringe frog front frost frown frozen f
gap garage garbage garden garlic garment gas gasp gate gather gauge gaze general genius genre g
d glance glare glass glide glimpse globe gloom glory glove glow glue goat goddess gold good goose g
ravity great green grid grief grit grocery group grow grunt guard guess guide guilt guitar gun gym habit
ave hawk hazard head health heart heavy hedgehog height hello helmet help hen hero hidden high hill I
hood hope horn horror horse hospital host hotel hour hover hub huge human humble humor hundred l
ignore ill illegal illness image imitate immense immune impact impose improve impulse inch include
le inherit initial inject injury inmate inner innocent input inquiry insane insect inside inspire install intact
cket jaguar jar jazz jealous jeans jelly jewel job join joke journey joy judge juice jump jungle junior junk
ss kit kitchen kite kitten kiwi knee knife knock know lab label labor ladder lady lake lamp language lap
er leaf learn leave lecture left leg legal legend leisure lemon lend length lens leopard lesson letter leve
little live lizard load loan lobster local lock logic lonely long loop lottery loud lounge love loyal lucky lu
id mail main major make mammal man manage mandate mango mansion manual maple marble march
th matrix matter maximum maze meadow mean measure meat mechanic medal media melody melt member n
ethod middle midnight milk million mimic mind minimum minor minute miracle mirror misery miss mis
nonkey monster month moon moral more morning mosquito mother motion motor mountain mouse m
c must mutual myself mystery myth naive name napkin narrow nasty nation nature near neck need nega
next nice night noble noise nominee noodle normal north nose notable note nothing notice novel nov
btain obvious occur ocean october odor off offer office often oil okay old olive olympic omit once one
ard order ordinary organ orient original orphan ostrich other outdoor outer output outside oval oven over
anda panel panic panther paper parade parent park parrot party pass patch path patient patrol pattern pa
cil people pepper perfect permit person pet phone photo phrase physical piano picnic picture piece pig p
plate play please pledge pluck plug plunge poem poet point polar pole police pond pony pool popular
practice praise predict prefer prepare present pretty prevent price pride primary print priority prison
proof property prosper protect proud provide public pudding pull pulp pulse pumpkin punch pupil pupp
tum quarter question quick quit quiz quote rabbit raccoon race rack radar radio rail rain raise rally ram
eal reason rebel rebuild recall receive recipe record recycle reduce reflect reform refuse region regret
e render renew rent reopen repair repeat replace report require rescue resemble resist resource respo
ribbon rice rich ride ridge rifle right rigid ring riot ripple risk ritual rival river road roast robot robust i
rubber rude rug rule run runway rural sad saddle sadness safe sail salad salmon salon salt salute sar
scare scatter scene scheme school science scissors scorpion scout scrap screen script scrub sea sear
cl sell seminar senior sense sentence series service session settle setup seven shadow shaft shallow sh
hop short shoulder shove shrimp shrug shuffle shy sibling sick side siege sight sign silent silk silly silve
skill skin skirt skull slab slam sleep slender slice slide slight slim slogan slot slow slush small smart s
ock soda soft solar soldier solid solution solve someone song soon sorry sort soul sound soup source s
ire spice spider spike spin spirit split spoil sponsor spoon sport spot spray spread spring spy square
tate stay steak steel stem step stereo stick still sting stock stomach stone stool story stove strategy st
bway success such sudden suffer sugar suggest suit summer sun sunny sunset super supply supreme
swamp swap swarm swear sweet swift swim swing switch sword symbol symptom syrup system tabl
h team tell ten tenant tennis tent term test text thank that theme then theory there they thing this tho
tiny tip tired tissue title toast tobacco today toddler toe together toilet token tomato tomorrow tone ton
tourist toward tower town toy track trade traffic tragic train transfer trap trash travel tray treat tree
rumpet trust truth try tube tuition tumble tuna tunnel turkey turn turtle twelve twenty twice twin twist
ndo unfair unfold unhappy uniform un... until unusual unveil update up
eless usual utility vacant vacuum vag... or various vast vault vehicle v
le vibrant vicious victory video view v... a visit visual vital vivid vocal v
ut want warfare warm warrior wash wasp waste water wave way wealth weapon wear weasel weather
el when where whip whisper wide width wife wild will win window wine wing wink winner winter wire

DAILY SEED

Wallet name
June 1

Derivation path
ot/exodus/3/5

SEED WORDS

1. God
2. said
3. to
4. him
5. do
6. not
7. come
8. any
9. closer
10. take
11. your
12. sandals

SEED WORDS

13. off
14. your
15. feet
16. the
17. place
18. where
19. you
20. are
21. standing
22. is
23. holy
24. ground

Wallet name
June 2

Derivation path
ot/psalm/103/14

SEED WORDS

1. for
2. he
3. knows
4. how
5. we
6. are
7. formed
8. he
9. remembers
10. that
11. we
12. are

Passphrase: _dust_

DAILY SEED

Wallet name
June 3

Derivation path
ot/job/26/7-10

SEED WORDS

1. he
2. hangs
3. the
4. earth
5. on
6. nothing
7. he
8. marks
9. out
10. the
11. horizon
12. on

SEED WORDS

13. the
14. face
15. of
16. the
17. waters
18. for
19. a
20. boundary
21. between
22. light
23. and
24. dark

DAILY SEED

Wallet name
June 4

Derivation path
ot/proverbs/19/4

SEED WORDS

1. wealth
2. attracts
3. many
4. friends
5. but
6. even
7. the
8. closest
9. ally
10. deserts
11. the
12. poor

> *Since we're all rich with bitcoins, or we will be once they're worth a million dollars like everyone expects, we ought to put some of this unearned wealth to good use.*
>
> - Hal Finney

DAILY SEED

Wallet name
June 5

Derivation path
nt/acts/10/15

SEED WORDS

1. a
2. voice
3. said
4. to
5. him
6. do
7. not
8. call
9. unclean
10. what
11. God
12. has

Passphrase: _cleansed_

 161

Wallet name
June 6

Derivation path
nt/luke/14/11

SEED WORDS

1. those
2. who
3. exalt
4. themselves
5. will
6. be
7. humbled
8. and
9. those
10. who
11. humble
12. themselves

Passphrase: _exalted_

Wallet name
June 7

Derivation path
nt/romans/12/6

SEED WORDS

1. we
2. have
3. different
4. gifts
5. according
6. to
7. the
8. grace
9. given
10. to
11. each
12. one

DAILY SEED

Wallet name
June 8

Derivation path
ot/1samuel/16/7

SEED WORDS

1. man
2. looks
3. at
4. the
5. outward
6. appearance
7. but
8. god
9. looks
10. at
11. the
12. heart

Wallet name
June 9

Derivation path
nt/2corinthians/3/12

SEED WORDS

1. therefore
2. since
3. we
4. have
5. such
6. a
7. hope
8. we
9. have
10. a
11. great
12. boldness

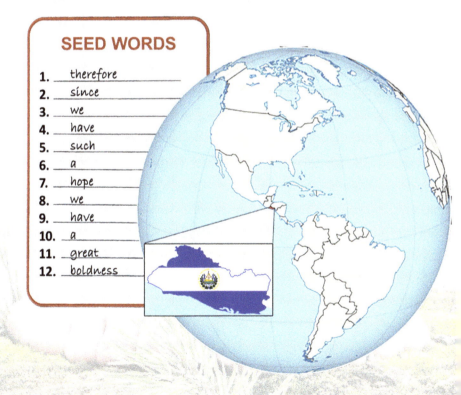

Wallet name
June 10

Derivation path
nt/titus/2/2

SEED WORDS

1. teach
2. the
3. older
4. men
5. to
6. be
7. temperate
8. worthy
9. of
10. respect
11. and
12. self-controlled

DAILY SEED

Wallet name
June 11

Derivation path
ot/proverbs/5/21

SEED WORDS

1. your
2. ways
3. are
4. in
5. full
6. view
7. of
8. the
9. lord
10. he
11. knows
12. your

Passphrase: paths

DAILY SEED

Wallet name
June 12

Derivation path
ot/isaiah/27/5

SEED WORDS

1. or
2. else
3. let
4. them
5. come
6. to
7. me
8. for
9. safety
10. and
11. refuge
12. let

SEED WORDS

13. them
14. make
15. peace
16. with
17. me
18. yes
19. let
20. them
21. make
22. peace
23. with
24. me

Wallet name
June 13

Derivation path
nt/matthew/8/1

SEED WORDS

1. when
2. jesus
3. came
4. down
5. from
6. the
7. mountain
8. large
9. crowds
10. followed
11. after
12. him

DAILY SEED

Wallet name
June 14

Derivation path
nt/colossians/1/15-16

SEED WORDS

1. the
2. son
3. is
4. the
5. image
6. of
7. the
8. invisible
9. god
10. the
11. firstborn
12. over

SEED WORDS

13. all
14. creation
15. in
16. him
17. all
18. things
19. were
20. created
21. in
22. heaven
23. and
24. earth

170

DAILY SEED

Wallet name
June 15

Derivation path
ot/psalm/22/1

SEED WORDS

1. my
2. god
3. my
4. god
5. why
6. have
7. you
8. forsaken
9. me
10. why
11. are
12. you

SEED WORDS

13. so
14. far
15. from
16. saving
17. me
18. so
19. far
20. from
21. my
22. cries
23. of
24. anguish

Wallet name
June 16

Derivation path
ot/psalm/23/6

SEED WORDS

1. surely
2. your
3. goodness
4. and
5. mercy
6. will
7. follow
8. me
9. all
10. of
11. my
12. days

DAILY SEED

Wallet name
June 17

Derivation path
nt/romans/1/2

SEED WORDS

1. the
2. gospel
3. he
4. promised
5. beforehand
6. through
7. his
8. prophets
9. in
10. the
11. holy
12. scriptures

Wallet name
June 18

Derivation path
nt/2peter/3/1

SEED WORDS

1. dear
2. friends
3. this
4. is
5. now
6. my
7. second
8. letter
9. to
10. you
11. i
12. have

SEED WORDS

13. written
14. them
15. both
16. as
17. reminders
18. to
19. stimulate
20. your
21. minds
22. to
23. wholesome
24. thinking

Wallet name
June 19

Derivation path
nt/hebrews/4/16

SEED WORDS

1. let
2. us
3. then
4. approach
5. god's
6. throne
7. of
8. grace
9. with
10. confidence
11. that
12. we

SEED WORDS

13. may
14. receive
15. mercy
16. and
17. find
18. grace
19. to
20. help
21. in
22. time
23. of
24. need

DAILY SEED

Wallet name
June 20

Derivation path
nt/jude/1/22-23

SEED WORDS

1. be
2. merciful
3. to
4. doubters
5. save
6. others
7. by
8. snatching
9. them
10. from
11. the
12. fire

Wallet name
June 21

Derivation path
nt/mark/12/43

SEED WORDS

1. i
2. tell
3. you
4. this
5. poor
6. widow
7. gave
8. more
9. than
10. all
11. the
12. others

Wallet name
June 22

Derivation path
nt/1john/4/2

SEED WORDS

1. every
2. spirit
3. that
4. acknowledges
5. jesus
6. christ
7. in
8. the
9. flesh
10. is
11. from
12. God

DAILY SEED

Wallet name
June 23

Derivation path
nt/ephesians/5/15

SEED WORDS

1. be
2. very
3. careful
4. then
5. how
6. you
7. live
8. not
9. as
10. unwise
11. but
12. as

SEED WORDS

13. wise
14. making
15. the
16. most
17. of
18. every
19. opportunity
20. because
21. the
22. days
23. are
24. evil

Wallet name
June 24

Derivation path
nt/1thessalonians/4/11

SEED WORDS

1. make
2. it
3. your
4. ambition
5. to
6. lead
7. a
8. quiet
9. life
10. you
11. should
12. mind

SEED WORDS

13. your
14. own
15. business
16. and
17. work
18. with
19. your
20. hands
21. just
22. as
23. we
24. instructed

Wallet name

June 25

Derivation path

ot/psalm/51/12

SEED WORDS

1. restore
2. unto
3. me
4. the
5. joy
6. of
7. your
8. salvation
9. and
10. uphold
11. my
12. spirit

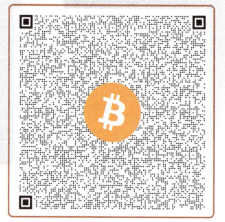

Wallet name
June 26

Derivation path
nt/1thessalonians/5/2

SEED WORDS

1. the
2. day
3. of
4. the
5. lord
6. will
7. come
8. like
9. a
10. thief
11. in
12. the

Passphrase: _night_

DAILY SEED

Wallet name
June 27

Derivation path
nt/mark/11/25

SEED WORDS

1. and
2. when
3. you
4. stand
5. praying
6. if
7. you
8. hold
9. anything
10. against
11. anyone
12. forgive

SEED WORDS

13. them
14. so
15. that
16. your
17. father
18. in
19. heaven
20. may
21. forgive
22. you
23. your
24. sins

DAILY SEED

Wallet name
June 28

Derivation path
ot/psalm/49/15

SEED WORDS

1. but
2. my
3. god
4. will
5. redeem
6. me
7. from
8. the
9. realm
10. of
11. the
12. dead

SEED WORDS

13. yes
14. he
15. will
16. surely
17. take
18. me
19. to
20. be
21. with
22. him
23. in
24. heaven

Wallet name
June 29

Derivation path
ot/psalm/102/11

SEED WORDS

1. my
2. days
3. are
4. like
5. the
6. evening
7. shadow
8. i
9. wither
10. away
11. like
12. grass

Wallet name
June 30

Derivation path
nt/mark/16/6

SEED WORDS

1. don't
2. be
3. alarmed
4. you
5. are
6. looking
7. for
8. jesus
9. who
10. was
11. crucified
12. he

SEED WORDS

13. has
14. risen
15. he
16. is
17. not
18. here
19. see
20. the
21. place
22. where
23. he
24. lay

DAILY SEED

Wallet name
July 1

Derivation path
nt/hebrews/13/3

SEED WORDS

1. continue
2. to
3. remember
4. those
5. in
6. prison
7. as
8. if
9. you
10. were
11. there
12. with

Passphrase: them

187

Wallet name
July 2

Derivation path
ot/psalm/51/16-17

SEED WORDS

1. you
2. do
3. not
4. take
5. pleasure
6. in
7. burnt
8. offerings
9. my
10. sacrifice
11. is
12. a

SEED WORDS

13. broken
14. spirit
15. and
16. a
17. broken
18. and
19. contrite
20. heart
21. you
22. will
23. not
24. despise

DAILY SEED

Wallet name
July 3

Derivation path
ot/psalm/102/25-26

SEED WORDS

1. in
2. the
3. beginning
4. you
5. laid
6. the
7. foundations
8. of
9. the
10. earth
11. and
12. the

SEED WORDS

13. heavens
14. are
15. the
16. work
17. of
18. your
19. hands
20. they
21. will
22. perish
23. but
24. you

Passphrase: remain

DAILY SEED

Wallet name
July 4

Derivation path
nt/ephesians/5/19-20

SEED WORDS

1. sing
2. and
3. make
4. music
5. from
6. your
7. heart
8. to
9. the
10. lord
11. always
12. giving

SEED WORDS

13. thanks
14. to
15. God
16. the
17. father
18. for
19. everything
20. through
21. our
22. lord
23. jesus
24. christ

DAILY SEED

Wallet name
July 5

Derivation path
nt/1thessalonians5/9-10

SEED WORDS

1. for
2. god
3. did
4. not
5. appoint
6. us
7. to
8. suffer
9. wrath
10. but
11. to
12. receive

SEED WORDS

13. salvation
14. through
15. our
16. lord
17. jesus
18. christ
19. he
20. died
21. so
22. we
23. may
24. live

DAILY SEED

Wallet name
July 6

Derivation path
nt/hebrews/12/2

SEED WORDS

1. fixing
2. our
3. eyes
4. on
5. jesus
6. the
7. author
8. and
9. perfector
10. of
11. our
12. faith

Wallet name

July 7

Derivation path

ot/psalm/49/20

SEED WORDS

1. people
2. that
3. have
4. wealth
5. but
6. lack
7. understanding
8. are
9. like
10. beasts
11. that
12. perish

DAILY SEED

Wallet name
July 8

Derivation path
nt/mark/12/30

SEED WORDS

1. brothers
2. love
3. the
4. lord
5. your
6. god
7. with
8. all
9. your
10. heart
11. and
12. all

SEED WORDS

13. your
14. soul
15. and
16. with
17. all
18. your
19. mind
20. and
21. with
22. all
23. your
24. strength

Wallet name
July 9

Derivation path
nt/phillipians/1/6

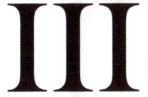

SEED WORDS

1. being
2. confident
3. that
4. he
5. who
6. has
7. begun
8. a
9. good
10. work
11. in
12. you

SEED WORDS

13. will
14. carry
15. it
16. through
17. to
18. completion
19. until
20. the
21. day
22. of
23. christ
24. jesus

DAILY SEED

Wallet name
July 10

Derivation path
nt/1john/4/9

SEED WORDS

1. in
2. this
3. the
4. love
5. of
6. god
7. was
8. made
9. manifest
10. that
11. god
12. sent

SEED WORDS

13. his
14. only
15. son
16. into
17. the
18. world
19. so
20. we
21. might
22. live
23. through
24. him

196

Wallet name
July 11

Derivation path
nt/romans/5/1

SEED WORDS

1. since
2. we
3. have
4. been
5. justified
6. by
7. faith
8. we
9. have
10. peace
11. with
12. God

DAILY **SEED**

Wallet name
July 12

Derivation path
nt/james/2/1

SEED WORDS

1. show
2. no
3. partiality
4. as
5. you
6. hold
7. the
8. faith
9. in
10. our
11. lord
12. jesus

Wallet name
July 13

Derivation path
nt/1john4/4

SEED WORDS

1. the
2. one
3. in
4. you
5. is
6. greater
7. than
8. the
9. one
10. in
11. the
12. world

Wallet name

July 14

Derivation path

nt/james2/5

SEED WORDS

1. listen
2. brothers
3. has
4. god
5. not
6. chosen
7. the
8. poor
9. in
10. this
11. world
12. to

SEED WORDS

13. be
14. rich
15. in
16. the
17. faith
18. and
19. heirs
20. of
21. the
22. kingdom
23. of
24. christ

Wallet name
July 15

Derivation path
ot/psalm/103/15-16

SEED WORDS

1. the
2. life
3. of
4. man
5. is
6. like
7. grass
8. like
9. a
10. flower
11. in
12. the

SEED WORDS

13. field
14. it
15. flourishes
16. the
17. wind
18. blows
19. over
20. it
21. and
22. it
23. is
24. gone

DAILY SEED

Wallet name
July 16

Derivation path
nt/2corinthians/10/5

SEED WORDS

1. we
2. demolish
3. arguments
4. and
5. every
6. pretension
7. that
8. sets
9. itself
10. up
11. against
12. the

SEED WORDS

13. knowledge
14. of
15. God
16. and
17. take
18. captive
19. every
20. thought
21. to
22. the
23. obedience
24. of

Passphrase: christ

202

Wallet name
July 17

Derivation path
nt/revelation/5/9

SEED WORDS

1. worthy
2. are
3. you
4. to
5. take
6. the
7. scroll
8. and
9. open
10. its
11. seals
12. for

SEED WORDS

13. you
14. were
15. slain
16. and
17. by
18. your
19. blood
20. you
21. ransomed
22. people
23. for
24. God

DAILY SEED

Wallet name
July 18

Derivation path
nt/hebrews/2/18

SEED WORDS

1. because
2. he
3. himself
4. was
5. tempted
6. he
7. is
8. able
9. to
10. help
11. those
12. being

Passphrase: tempted

Wallet name
July 19

Derivation path
nt/2peter/2/1

SEED WORDS

1. but
2. false
3. teachers
4. arose
5. among
6. the
7. people
8. who
9. secretly
10. taught
11. false
12. heresies

Wallet name
July 20

Derivation path
nt/hebrews/12/1

SEED WORDS

1. throw
2. off
3. everything
4. that
5. hinders
6. and
7. the
8. sin
9. that
10. so
11. easily
12. entangles

Wallet name
July 21

Derivation path
ot/malachi/3/3

SEED WORDS

1. he
2. will
3. refine
4. them
5. like
6. gold
7. and
8. purge
9. them
10. like
11. silver
12. and

SEED WORDS

13. then
14. the
15. lord
16. will
17. have
18. men
19. who
20. will
21. bring
22. offerings
23. in
24. righteousness

DAILY SEED

Wallet name
July 22

Derivation path
nt/1john/4/18

SEED WORDS

1. there
2. is
3. no
4. fear
5. in
6. love
7. because
8. perfect
9. love
10. casts
11. out
12. all

SEED WORDS

13. fear
14. the
15. one
16. who
17. fears
18. is
19. not
20. yet
21. made
22. perfect
23. in
24. love

208

DAILY SEED

Wallet name
July 23

Derivation path
nt/1peter/4/4

SEED WORDS

1. they
2. are
3. surprised
4. you
5. do
6. not
7. join
8. them
9. in
10. their
11. reckless
12. wild

Passphrase: living

209

DAILY SEED

Wallet name
July 24

Derivation path
nt/ephesians/5/21

SEED WORDS

1. submit
2. to
3. one
4. another
5. out
6. of
7. reverence
8. for
9. our
10. lord
11. jesus
12. christ

Wallet name
July 25

Derivation path
nt/mark/16/11-12

SEED WORDS

1. when
2. they
3. heard
4. that
5. jesus
6. was
7. alive
8. and
9. that
10. she
11. had
12. seen

SEED WORDS

13. him
14. they
15. did
16. not
17. believe
18. it
19. but
20. afterward
21. jesus
22. appeared
23. to
24. them

DAILY SEED

Wallet name
July 26

Derivation path
nt/mark/16/15-16

SEED WORDS

1. go
2. into
3. all
4. the
5. world
6. and
7. preach
8. the
9. gospel
10. he
11. who
12. believes

SEED WORDS

13. will
14. be
15. saved
16. but
17. he
18. who
19. does
20. not
21. believe
22. will
23. be
24. condemned

DAILY SEED

Wallet name
July 27

Derivation path
nt/1peter/4/8

SEED WORDS

1. love
2. each
3. other
4. deeply
5. because
6. love
7. covers
8. over
9. a
10. multitude
11. of
12. sins

Wallet name
July 28

Derivation path
nt/hebrews/4/29

SEED WORDS

1. let
2. no
3. unwholesome
4. speech
5. come
6. from
7. your
8. mouth
9. but
10. only
11. that
12. which

SEED WORDS

13. is
14. good
15. for
16. building
17. up
18. as
19. fits
20. the
21. occasion
22. full
23. of
24. grace

Wallet name
July 29

Derivation path
nt/philippians/3/1

SEED WORDS

1. writing
2. the
3. same
4. things
5. is
6. easy
7. for
8. me
9. and
10. a
11. safeguard
12. for

Passphrase: _you_

Wallet name
July 30

Derivation path
nt/1peter/4/12

SEED WORDS

1. do
2. not
3. be
4. surprised
5. at
6. the
7. fiery
8. ordeal
9. that
10. has
11. come
12. upon

SEED WORDS

13. you
14. to
15. test
16. you
17. as
18. though
19. something
20. strange
21. is
22. happening
23. to
24. you

DAILY SEED

Wallet name
July 31

Derivation path
nt/1thessalonians/5/15

SEED WORDS

1. make
2. sure
3. no
4. one
5. pays
6. back
7. wrong
8. for
9. wrong
10. but
11. always
12. strives

SEED WORDS

13. to
14. do
15. what
16. is
17. good
18. for
19. each
20. other
21. and
22. for
23. everyone
24. else

217

Wallet name
August 1

Derivation path
ot/isaiah/53/1

SEED WORDS

1. who
2. has
3. believed
4. our
5. report
6. to
7. whom
8. has
9. our
10. message
11. been
12. revealed

For the next 12 days we will read Isaiah 53. Written about 700 years before the birth of Christ, this prophesy describes in stunning detail the ministry of Jesus, touching on his upbringing, the manner of his death and burial, and foretelling his resurrection. Beyond these details, the prophesy also answers why he did it all. Many details have been left out of these seed phrases, so I urge you to read it from a Bible.

DAILY SEED

Wallet name
August 2

Derivation path
ot/isaiah/53/2

SEED WORDS

1. when
2. we
3. see
4. him
5. he
6. had
7. no
8. beauty
9. or
10. majesty
11. to
12. attract

SEED WORDS

13. us
14. to
15. him
16. nothing
17. in
18. his
19. appearance
20. that
21. we
22. should
23. desire
24. him

220

Wallet name
August 3

Derivation path
ot/isaiah/53/3

SEED WORDS

1. he
2. was
3. despised
4. and
5. rejected
6. by
7. men
8. he
9. was
10. a
11. man
12. of

SEED WORDS

13. sorrow
14. familiar
15. with
16. pain
17. he
18. was
19. despised
20. and
21. held
22. in
23. low
24. esteem

DAILY SEED

Wallet name
August 4

Derivation path
ot/isaiah/53/4

SEED WORDS

1. surely
2. he
3. has
4. borne
5. our
6. griefs
7. and
8. carried
9. our
10. suffering
11. but
12. yet

SEED WORDS

13. we
14. considered
15. him
16. punished
17. by
18. God
19. and
20. stricken
21. by
22. him
23. and
24. afflicted

222

DAILY SEED

Wallet name
August 5

Derivation path
ot/isaiah/53/5

SEED WORDS

1. but
2. he
3. was
4. pierced
5. for
6. our
7. transgressions
8. and
9. the
10. punishment
11. that
12. brought

SEED WORDS

13. us
14. peace
15. was
16. upon
17. him
18. and
19. by
20. his
21. wounds
22. we
23. are
24. healed

Wallet name
August 6

Derivation path
ot/isaiah/53/6

SEED WORDS

1. we
2. all
3. like
4. sheep
5. have
6. gone
7. astray
8. each
9. to
10. his
11. own
12. way

SEED WORDS

13. and
14. the
15. lord
16. has
17. laid
18. on
19. him
20. the
21. iniquity
22. of
23. us
24. all

DAILY SEED

Wallet name
August 7

Derivation path
ot/isaiah/53/7

SEED WORDS

1. he
2. was
3. led
4. as
5. a
6. lamb
7. to
8. the
9. slaughter
10. and
11. as
12. a

SEED WORDS

13. sheep
14. is
15. silent
16. before
17. its
18. sheerer
19. so
20. he
21. didn't
22. open
23. his
24. mouth

225

DAILY SEED

Wallet name
August 8

Derivation path
ot/isaiah/53/8

SEED WORDS

1. by
2. oppression
3. and
4. judgement
5. he
6. was
7. taken
8. cut
9. off
10. from
11. the
12. land

SEED WORDS

13. of
14. the
15. living
16. for
17. the
18. sins
19. of
20. my
21. people
22. he
23. was
24. punished

Wallet name
August 9

Derivation path
ot/isaiah/53/9

SEED WORDS

1. he
2. was
3. assigned
4. a
5. grave
6. with
7. the
8. wicked
9. and
10. with
11. the
12. rich

SEED WORDS

13. in
14. his
15. death
16. though
17. he
18. had
19. done
20. no
21. violence
22. nor
23. deceived
24. anyone

227

DAILY SEED

Wallet name
August 10

Derivation path
ot/isaiah/53/10

SEED WORDS

1. yet
2. it
3. was
4. the
5. lord's
6. will
7. to
8. crush
9. him
10. and
11. cause
12. him

SEED WORDS

13. to
14. suffer
15. and
16. to
17. make
18. his
19. life
20. an
21. offering
22. for
23. our
24. sin

DAILY SEED

Wallet name
August 11

Derivation path
ot/isaiah/53/11

SEED WORDS

1. after
2. he
3. has
4. suffered
5. he
6. will
7. again
8. see
9. the
10. light
11. of
12. life

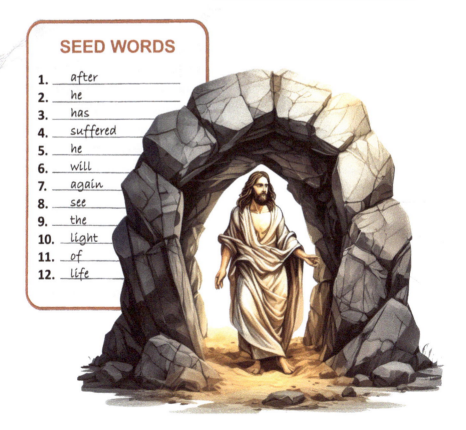

Wallet name
August 12

Derivation path
ot/isaiah/53/12

SEED WORDS

1. therefore
2. i
3. will
4. give
5. him
6. a
7. portion
8. among
9. the
10. great
11. because
12. he

SEED WORDS

13. poured
14. out
15. his
16. life
17. unto
18. death
19. and
20. was
21. numbered
22. among
23. the
24. transgressors

Wallet name
August 13

Derivation path
nt/john/8/32

SEED WORDS

1. you
2. shall
3. know
4. the
5. truth
6. and
7. the
8. truth
9. will
10. set
11. you
12. free

Wallet name
August 14

Derivation path
nt/galatians/5/1

SEED WORDS

1. it
2. is
3. for
4. the
5. sake
6. of
7. freedom
8. that
9. christ
10. set
11. us
12. free

Wallet name	Derivation path
August 15	ot/deuteronomy/32/35

SEED WORDS

1. vengeance
2. is
3. mine
4. says
5. the
6. lord
7. their
8. doom
9. comes
10. upon
11. them
12. quickly

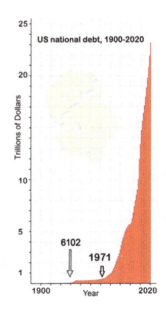

US national debt, 1900-2020

Trillions of Dollars

6102

1971

1900   Year   2020

Wallet name
August 16

Derivation path
nt/john/6/40

SEED WORDS

1. everyone
2. who
3. looks
4. to
5. the
6. son
7. and
8. believes
9. in
10. him
11. shall
12. live

Passphrase: forever

Wallet name
August 17

Derivation path
ot/2samuel/19/6

SEED WORDS

1. you
2. love
3. those
4. who
5. hate
6. you
7. and
8. hate
9. those
10. who
11. love
12. you

DAILY SEED

Wallet name
August 18

Derivation path
ot/psalm/64/10

SEED WORDS

1. let
2. the
3. righteous
4. rejoice
5. in
6. the
7. lord
8. and
9. take
10. refuge
11. in
12. him

Wallet name
August 19

Derivation path
nt/1peter/4/16

SEED WORDS

1. if
2. you
3. suffer
4. as
5. a
6. christian
7. don't
8. be
9. ashamed
10. but
11. praise
12. God

Wallet name
August 20

Derivation path
nt/ephesians/6/11

SEED WORDS

1. put
2. on
3. the
4. full
5. armor
6. of
7. God
8. so
9. that
10. you
11. may
12. be

SEED WORDS

13. able
14. to
15. stand
16. strong
17. against
18. the
19. schemes
20. of
21. our
22. enemy
23. the
24. devil

Wallet name
August 21

Derivation path
nt/revelation/6/6

SEED WORDS

1. a
2. quart
3. of
4. wheat
5. for
6. a
7. day's
8. wages
9. and
10. three
11. quarts
12. of

SEED WORDS

13. barley
14. for
15. a
16. day's
17. wages
18. and
19. don't
20. harm
21. the
22. oil
23. or
24. wine

DAILY SEED

Wallet name
August 22

Derivation path
ot/1samuel/19/24

SEED WORDS

1. he
2. stripped
3. off
4. his
5. clothes
6. and
7. he
8. too
9. prophesied
10. before
11. samuel
12. he

SEED WORDS

13. lay
14. naked
15. all
16. day
17. and
18. all
19. night
20. is
21. saul
22. also
23. a
24. prophet

Wallet name
August 23

Derivation path
nt/1peter/2/8

SEED WORDS

1. now
2. to
3. you
4. who
5. believe
6. this
7. stone
8. is
9. precious
10. but
11. those
12. who

SEED WORDS

13. do
14. not
15. believe
16. the
17. stone
18. the
19. builders
20. rejected
21. has
22. become
23. the
24. cornerstone

Wallet name
August 24

Derivation path
ot/genesis/1/27

SEED WORDS

1. God
2. created
3. man
4. in
5. his
6. image
7. in
8. the
9. image
10. of
11. God
12. he

SEED WORDS

13. created
14. him
15. male
16. and
17. female
18. he
19. created
20. them
21. and
22. he
23. blessed
24. them

Wallet name
August 25

Derivation path
nt/ephesians/6/12

SEED WORDS

1. for
2. our
3. struggle
4. is
5. not
6. against
7. flesh
8. and
9. blood
10. but
11. against
12. powers

SEED WORDS

13. and
14. principalities
15. and
16. the
17. spiritual
18. forces
19. of
20. evil
21. in
22. the
23. heavenly
24. realms

Wallet name
August 26

Derivation path
ot/psalm/103/8

SEED WORDS

1. the
2. lord
3. is
4. merciful
5. and
6. gracious
7. slow
8. to
9. anger
10. abounding
11. in
12. love

DAILY SEED

Wallet name
August 27

Derivation path
nt/romans/3/23

SEED WORDS

1. for
2. all
3. have
4. sinned
5. and
6. fallen
7. short
8. of
9. the
10. glory
11. of
12. God

For the remainder of August we will travel down Roman's Road of Salvation. This 'road' consists of several verses in the book of Romans that succinctly give the gospel message, beginning with today's verse:

Romans 3:23

DAILY **SEED**

Wallet name
August 28

Derivation path
nt/romans/6/23

SEED WORDS

1. the
2. wages
3. of
4. sin
5. is
6. death
7. the
8. gift
9. of
10. God
11. is
12. eternal

Passphrase: ___life___

DAILY SEED

Wallet name
August 29

Derivation path
nt/romans/10/9

SEED WORDS

1. if
2. you
3. confess
4. with
5. your
6. mouth
7. jesus
8. is
9. lord
10. and
11. believe
12. in

SEED WORDS

13. your
14. heart
15. that
16. God
17. raised
18. him
19. from
20. death
21. you
22. will
23. be
24. saved

Wallet name
August 30

Derivation path
nt/romans/8/1

SEED WORDS

1. there
2. is
3. now
4. no
5. condemnation
6. for
7. those
8. who
9. are
10. in
11. christ
12. jesus

Wallet name
August 31

Derivation path
nt/romans/8/38-39

SEED WORDS

1. for
2. i
3. am
4. convinced
5. that
6. nothing
7. in
8. all
9. creation
10. can
11. separate
12. us

SEED WORDS

13. from
14. the
15. love
16. of
17. God
18. that
19. is
20. in
21. christ
22. jesus
23. our
24. lord

DAILY SEED

Wallet name
September 1

Derivation path
nt/1john/4/6

SEED WORDS

1. we
2. are
3. from
4. God
5. and
6. whoever
7. is
8. from
9. God
10. listens
11. to
12. us

Wallet name
September 2

Derivation path
ot/psalm/51/1-2

SEED WORDS

1. have
2. mercy
3. on
4. me
5. my
6. God
7. according
8. to
9. your
10. unfailing
11. love
12. according

SEED WORDS

13. to
14. your
15. great
16. compassion
17. blot
18. out
19. my
20. trangressions
21. wash
22. away
23. my
24. iniquity

Wallet name
September 3

Derivation path
nt/john/6/38

SEED WORDS

1. for
2. i
3. have
4. not
5. come
6. down
7. from
8. heaven
9. to
10. do
11. my
12. own

SEED WORDS

13. will
14. but
15. to
16. do
17. the
18. will
19. of
20. my
21. father
22. that
23. sent
24. me

Wallet name
September 4

Derivation path
nt/romans/14/1

SEED WORDS

1. welcome
2. the
3. weak
4. in
5. the
6. faith
7. and
8. do
9. not
10. quarrel
11. over
12. opinions

Wallet name
September 5

Derivation path
nt/mark/15/37-38

SEED WORDS

1. then
2. jesus
3. called
4. out
5. with
6. a
7. loud
8. voice
9. and
10. breathed
11. his
12. last

SEED WORDS

13. and
14. the
15. temple
16. curtain
17. was
18. torn
19. in
20. two
21. from
22. top
23. to
24. bottom

Wallet name
September 6

Derivation path
nt/acts/1/9

SEED WORDS

1. now
2. after
3. he
4. had
5. finished
6. speaking
7. these
8. things
9. he
10. was
11. taken
12. up

SEED WORDS

13. before
14. their
15. very
16. eyes
17. and
18. a
19. cloud
20. hid
21. him
22. from
23. their
24. sight

Wallet name
September 7

Derivation path
ot/proverbs/21/6

SEED WORDS

1. fortunes
2. made
3. by
4. a
5. lying
6. tongue
7. are
8. a
9. fleeting
10. vapor
11. a
12. deadly

Passphrase: _snare_

DAILY SEED

Wallet name
September 8

Derivation path
nt/1timothy/6/17

SEED WORDS

1. instruct
2. the
3. rich
4. not
5. to
6. be
7. arrogant
8. or
9. put
10. their
11. hope
12. in

SEED WORDS

13. wealth
14. which
15. is
16. so
17. uncertain
18. but
19. in
20. God
21. who
22. so
23. richly
24. provides

258

Wallet name
September 9

Derivation path
nt/1timothy/6/18-19

SEED WORDS

1. command
2. them
3. to
4. be
5. rich
6. in
7. good
8. deeds
9. always
10. being
11. generous
12. and

SEED WORDS

13. willing
14. to
15. share
16. freely
17. thereby
18. storing
19. up
20. for
21. themselves
22. treasure
23. in
24. heaven

Wallet name
September 10

Derivation path
nt/1peter/1/8

SEED WORDS

1. though
2. you
3. have
4. not
5. seen
6. him
7. you
8. love
9. him
10. and
11. believe
12. in

Passphrase: _____him_____

DAILY SEED

Wallet name
September 11

Derivation path
ot/proverbs/3/25

SEED WORDS

1. be
2. not
3. afraid
4. of
5. sudden
6. terror
7. nor
8. the
9. attack
10. of
11. the
12. wicked

Wallet name
September 12

Derivation path
nt/2john/1/6

SEED WORDS

1. and
2. this
3. is
4. love
5. that
6. we
7. walk
8. in
9. obedience
10. to
11. his
12. commands

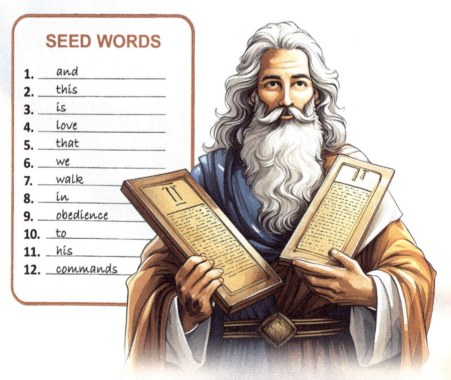

DAILY SEED

Wallet name
September 13

Derivation path
ot/psalm/34/8-9

SEED WORDS

1. taste
2. and
3. see
4. that
5. the
6. lord
7. is
8. good
9. blessed
10. is
11. the
12. man

SEED WORDS

13. who
14. puts
15. his
16. trust
17. in
18. him
19. fear
20. the
21. lord
22. you
23. his
24. saints

Wallet name
September 14

Derivation path
ot/proverbs/22/4

SEED WORDS

1. humility
2. is
3. the
4. fear
5. of
6. the
7. lord
8. its
9. wages
10. are
11. riches
12. and

Passphrase: life

DAILY SEED

Wallet name
September 15

Derivation path
ot/proverbs/22/3

SEED WORDS

1. the
2. prudent
3. see
4. danger
5. and
6. flee
7. the
8. simple
9. continue
10. and
11. pay
12. the

Passphrase: penalty

Wallet name
September 16

Derivation path
ot/psalm/106/3

SEED WORDS

1. blessed
2. are
3. those
4. who
5. act
6. justly
7. who
8. always
9. do
10. what
11. is
12. right

Wallet name
September 17

Derivation path
ot/psalm/34/12

SEED WORDS

1. my
2. children
3. if
4. you
5. love
6. life
7. and
8. desire
9. to
10. see
11. many
12. good

SEED WORDS

13. days
14. keep
15. your
16. tongue
17. from
18. evil
19. and
20. your
21. lips
22. from
23. telling
24. lies

267

Wallet name
September 18

Derivation path
ot/isaiah/6/8

SEED WORDS

1. the
2. voice
3. of
4. the
5. lord
6. said
7. whom
8. shall
9. i
10. send
11. and
12. who

SEED WORDS

13. will
14. go
15. for
16. us
17. then
18. i
19. said
20. here
21. i
22. am
23. send
24. me

Wallet name
September 19

Derivation path
nt/john/7/24

SEED WORDS

1. do
2. not
3. judge
4. by
5. mere
6. appearances
7. but
8. learn
9. to
10. judge
11. with
12. righteous

Passphrase: judgment

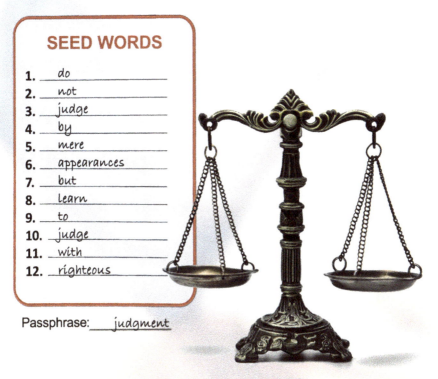

DAILY SEED

Wallet name
September 20

Derivation path
nt/revelation/13/17

SEED WORDS

1. no
2. one
3. was
4. allowed
5. to
6. buy
7. or
8. sell
9. without
10. the
11. mark
12. which

SEED WORDS

13. is
14. the
15. name
16. of
17. the
18. beast
19. or
20. the
21. number
22. of
23. its
24. name

DAILY SEED

Wallet name
September 21

Derivation path
nt/revelation/14/9-10

SEED WORDS

1. if
2. anyone
3. received
4. the
5. mark
6. of
7. the
8. beast
9. they
10. too
11. will
12. drink

SEED WORDS

13. the
14. wine
15. of
16. God's
17. fury
18. poured
19. into
20. the
21. cup
22. of
23. his
24. wrath

DAILY SEED

Wallet name
September 22

Derivation path
nt/revelation/20/4

SEED WORDS

1. they
2. came
3. to
4. life
5. and
6. reigned
7. with
8. christ
9. for
10. one
11. thousand
12. years

Wallet name
September 23

Derivation path
nt/revelation/21/18

SEED WORDS

1. the
2. wall
3. was
4. made
5. of
6. jasper
7. and
8. the
9. city
10. of
11. pure
12. gold

DAILY SEED

Wallet name
September 24

Derivation path
ot/psalm/41/1

SEED WORDS

1. blessed
2. is
3. he
4. who
5. considers
6. the
7. poor
8. the
9. lord
10. will
11. deliver
12. him

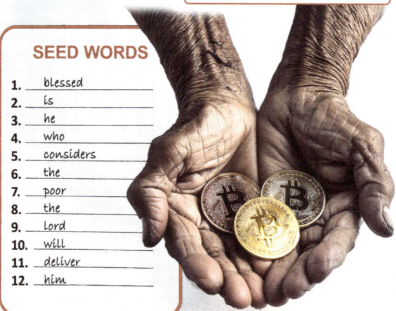

DAILY SEED

Wallet name
September 25

Derivation path
ot/proverbs/6/6

SEED WORDS

1. consider
2. the
3. ant
4. and
5. be
6. wise
7. it
8. has
9. no
10. commander
11. or
12. leader

SEED WORDS

13. or
14. ruler
15. yet
16. it
17. gathers
18. at
19. harvest
20. and
21. stores
22. provisions
23. in
24. summer

Wallet name
September 26

Derivation path
ot/isaiah/6/9

SEED WORDS

1. be
2. ever
3. hearing
4. but
5. never
6. understanding
7. be
8. ever
9. seeing
10. but
11. never
12. perceiving

Wallet name
September 27

Derivation path
nt/mark/16/14

SEED WORDS

1. later
2. jesus
3. appeared
4. to
5. the
6. eleven
7. as
8. they
9. were
10. eating
11. and
12. he

SEED WORDS

13. rebuked
14. them
15. for
16. their
17. lack
18. of
19. faith
20. and
21. stubborn
22. refusal
23. to
24. believe

Wallet name
September 28

Derivation path
nt/john/20/25

SEED WORDS

1. but
2. he
3. said
4. unless
5. i
6. see
7. the
8. nail
9. marks
10. in
11. his
12. hand

SEED WORDS

13. and
14. put
15. my
16. fingers
17. where
18. the
19. nails
20. were
21. i
22. will
23. not
24. believe

DAILY SEED

Wallet name
September 29

Derivation path
ot/psalm/34/14

SEED WORDS

1. turn
2. from
3. evil
4. and
5. do
6. good
7. seek
8. peace
9. and
10. hotly
11. pursue
12. it

DAILY SEED

Wallet name
September 30

Derivation path
ot/proverbs/21/20

SEED WORDS

1. the
2. wise
3. store
4. up
5. choice
6. food
7. but
8. the
9. fool
10. gulps
11. it
12. down

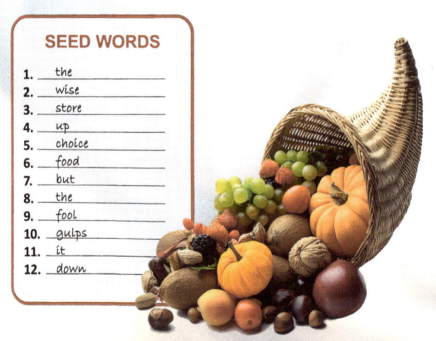

DAILY SEED

Wallet name
October 1

Derivation path
nt/1john/4/8

SEED WORDS

1. whoever
2. does
3. not
4. love
5. does
6. not
7. know
8. God
9. because
10. God
11. is
12. love

Wallet name
October 2

Derivation path
ot/psalm/51/10

SEED WORDS

1. create
2. in
3. me
4. a
5. pure
6. heart
7. renew
8. a
9. right
10. spirit
11. within
12. me

DAILY SEED

Wallet name
October 3

Derivation path
nt/john/8/7

SEED WORDS

1. let
2. him
3. who
4. is
5. without
6. sin
7. be
8. the
9. first
10. to
11. cast
12. a

Passphrase: stone

DAILY SEED

Wallet name
October 4

Derivation path
nt/john/8/10

SEED WORDS

1. woman
2. where
3. are
4. your
5. accusers
6. has
7. no
8. one
9. stayed
10. to
11. accuse
12. you

DAILY SEED

Wallet name
October 5

Derivation path
nt/john/3/17

SEED WORDS

1. for
2. God
3. did
4. not
5. send
6. his
7. only
8. son
9. into
10. the
11. world
12. to

SEED WORDS

13. condemn
14. the
15. world
16. but
17. that
18. the
19. world
20. through
21. him
22. might
23. be
24. saved

285

DAILY SEED

Wallet name
October 6

Derivation path
nt/1peter/1/18-19

SEED WORDS

1. for
2. you
3. were
4. not
5. redeemed
6. by
7. perishable
8. things
9. like
10. silver
11. or
12. gold

SEED WORDS

13. but
14. by
15. the
16. precious
17. blood
18. of
19. jesus
20. christ
21. a
22. lamb
23. without
24. blemish

DAILY SEED

Wallet name
October 7

Derivation path
nt/john/6/58

SEED WORDS

1. your
2. fathers
3. ate
4. manna
5. from
6. heaven
7. and
8. died
9. i
10. am
11. the
12. living

SEED WORDS

13. bread
14. that
15. came
16. from
17. heaven
18. whoever
19. eats
20. this
21. bread
22. will
23. live
24. forever

287

DAILY SEED

Wallet name
October 8

Derivation path
nt/romans/14/8

SEED WORDS

1. if
2. we
3. live
4. we
5. live
6. to
7. the
8. lord
9. and
10. if
11. we
12. die

SEED WORDS

13. we
14. die
15. to
16. the
17. lord
18. either
19. way
20. we
21. belong
22. to
23. the
24. lord

DAILY SEED

Wallet name
October 9

Derivation path
ot/proverbs/16/22

SEED WORDS

1. a
2. man
3. seems
4. right
5. in
6. his
7. eyes
8. but
9. God
10. weighs
11. the
12. motives

289

DAILY SEED

Wallet name
October 10

Derivation path
ot/psalm/106/20

SEED WORDS

1. they
2. exchanged
3. their
4. glorious
5. god
6. for
7. image
8. of
9. bull
10. that
11. eats
12. grass

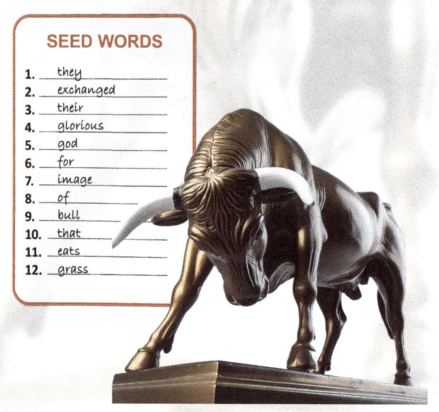

Wallet name
October 11

Derivation path
nt/john/1/30

SEED WORDS

1. he
2. who
3. came
4. after
5. me
6. has
7. surpassed
8. me
9. because
10. he
11. was
12. before

Passphrase: me

Wallet name
October 12

Derivation path
ot/proverbs/18/11

SEED WORDS

1. a
2. rich
3. man's
4. wealth
5. is
6. a
7. citadel
8. a
9. high
10. wall
11. in
12. his

Passphrase: imagination

DAILY SEED

Wallet name
October 13

Derivation path
ot/proverbs/22/2

SEED WORDS

1. rich
2. and
3. poor
4. have
5. this
6. in
7. common
8. the
9. Lord
10. is
11. maker
12. of

Passphrase: both

293

Wallet name
October 14

Derivation path
nt/1corinthians/13/4

SEED WORDS

1. love
2. is
3. patient
4. love
5. is
6. kind
7. it
8. does
9. not
10. envy
11. or
12. boast

DAILY SEED

Wallet name
October 15

Derivation path
nt/1corinthians/13/5

SEED WORDS

1. love
2. is
3. not
4. dishonoring
5. to
6. others
7. it
8. is
9. not
10. self-seeking
11. it
12. is

SEED WORDS

13. not
14. easily
15. angered
16. and
17. it
18. does
19. not
20. keep
21. a
22. record
23. of
24. wrongs

295

DAILY SEED

Wallet name
October 16

Derivation path
nt/1corinthians/13/6-8

SEED WORDS

1. love
2. does
3. not
4. delight
5. in
6. evil
7. but
8. rejoices
9. in
10. the
11. truth
12. love

SEED WORDS

13. bears
14. all
15. things
16. hopes
17. all
18. things
19. endures
20. all
21. things
22. love
23. never
24. fails

296

Wallet name
October 17

Derivation path
nt/galatians/4/16

SEED WORDS

1. have
2. i
3. now
4. become
5. your
6. enemy
7. because
8. i
9. tell
10. you
11. the
12. truth

Wallet name
October 18

Derivation path
ot/psalm/41/9

SEED WORDS

1. even
2. my
3. close
4. friend
5. in
6. whom
7. i
8. trusted
9. and
10. shared
11. my
12. bread

SEED WORDS

13. has
14. turned
15. against
16. me
17. but
18. may
19. the
20. lord
21. have
22. mercy
23. on
24. me

Wallet name
October 19

Derivation path
nt/philippians/4/19

SEED WORDS

1. God
2. will
3. supply
4. all
5. your
6. needs
7. according
8. to
9. the
10. riches
11. of
12. his

Passphrase: glory

Wallet name
October 20

Derivation path
nt/revelation/1/3

SEED WORDS

1. blessed
2. is
3. the
4. one
5. who
6. reads
7. aloud
8. the
9. words
10. of
11. this
12. prophecy

SEED WORDS

13. and
14. blessed
15. are
16. those
17. who
18. hear
19. it
20. and
21. take
22. it
23. to
24. heart

300

Wallet name
October 21

Derivation path
ot/psalm/103/9

SEED WORDS

1. he
2. will
3. not
4. stay
5. angry
6. with
7. us
8. forever
9. he
10. does
11. not
12. treat

SEED WORDS

13. us
14. as
15. our
16. sins
17. deserve
18. or
19. repay
20. us
21. according
22. to
23. our
24. iniquities

DAILY SEED

Wallet name
October 22

Derivation path
nt/acts/20/29

SEED WORDS

1. know
2. that
3. after
4. my
5. departing
6. savage
7. wolves
8. will
9. come
10. in
11. among
12. you

Wallet name
October 23

Derivation path
nt/1peter/2/2

SEED WORDS

1. like
2. newborn
3. babes
4. crave
5. pure
6. spiritual
7. milk
8. that
9. you
10. may
11. grow
12. up

Wallet name
October 24

Derivation path
nt/galatians/4/7

SEED WORDS

1. you
2. are
3. no
4. longer
5. a
6. slave
7. but
8. a
9. child
10. of
11. God
12. and

SEED WORDS

13. since
14. you
15. are
16. his
17. child
18. God
19. has
20. also
21. made
22. you
23. an
24. heir

Wallet name
October 25

Derivation path
nt/1thessalonians/5/5

SEED WORDS

1. you
2. are
3. children
4. of
5. the
6. light
7. and
8. you
9. are
10. children
11. of
12. the

SEED WORDS

13. day
14. we
15. do
16. not
17. belong
18. to
19. the
20. night
21. or
22. to
23. the
24. darkness

Wallet name
October 26

Derivation path
ot/psalm/42/2

SEED WORDS

1. my
2. soul
3. thirsts
4. for
5. God
6. when
7. may
8. i
9. go
10. meet
11. with
12. him

Wallet name
October 27

Derivation path
nt/1corinthians/15/14'17

SEED WORDS

1. if
2. christ
3. is
4. not
5. risen
6. our
7. preaching
8. is
9. useless
10. as
11. is
12. your

SEED WORDS

13. faith
14. if
15. christ
16. is
17. not
18. raised
19. you
20. are
21. still
22. in
23. your
24. sins

Wallet name
October 28

Derivation path
nt/luke/5/8

SEED WORDS

1. when
2. he
3. saw
4. it
5. simon
6. peter
7. fell
8. at
9. the
10. knees
11. of
12. jesus

SEED WORDS

13. and
14. said
15. go
16. away
17. from
18. me
19. lord
20. i
21. am
22. a
23. sinful
24. man

DAILY SEED

Wallet name
October 29

Derivation path
nt/1corinthians/13/13

SEED WORDS

1. and
2. now
3. abide
4. faith
5. hope
6. and
7. love
8. but
9. the
10. greatest
11. is
12. love

DAILY SEED

Wallet name
October 30

Derivation path
nt/matthew/13/44

SEED WORDS

1. the
2. kingdom
3. of
4. heaven
5. is
6. like
7. great
8. treasure
9. hidden
10. in
11. a
12. field

SEED WORDS

13. when
14. a
15. man
16. discovered
17. it
18. he
19. sold
20. everything
21. to
22. buy
23. that
24. field

DAILY SEED

Wallet name
October 31

Derivation path
ot/psalm/60/12

SEED WORDS

1. with
2. God
3. we
4. will
5. gain
6. the
7. victory
8. he
9. will
10. trample
11. down
12. our

Passphrase: enemies

Bitcoin: A Peer-to-Peer Electronic Cash System

Satoshi Nakamoto • satoshin@gmx.com • www.bitcoin.org

Abstract. A purely peer-to-peer version of electronic cash would allow online payments to be sent directly from one party to another without going through a financial institution. Digital signatures provide part of the solution, but the main benefits are lost if a trusted third party is still required to prevent double-spending. We propose a solution to the double-spending problem using a peer-to-peer network. The network timestamps transactions by hashing them into an ongoing chain of hash-based proof-of-work, forming a record that cannot be changed without redoing the proof-of-work. The longest chain not only serves as proof of the sequence of events witnessed, but proof that it came from the largest pool of CPU power. As long as a majority of CPU power is controlled by nodes that are not cooperating to attack the network, they'll generate the longest chain and outpace attackers. The network itself requires minimal structure. Messages are broadcast on a best effort basis, and nodes can leave and rejoin the network at will, accepting the longest proof-of-work chain as proof of what happened while they were gone.

DAILY SEED

Wallet name
November 1

Derivation path
ot/psalm/103/11

SEED WORDS

1. for
2. as
3. high
4. as
5. the
6. heavens
7. are
8. above
9. the
10. earth
11. so
12. great

SEED WORDS

13. is
14. his
15. love
16. and
17. mercy
18. toward
19. those
20. who
21. fear
22. his
23. holy
24. name

Wallet name
November 2

Derivation path
ot/psalm/103/12

SEED WORDS

1. for
2. as
3. far
4. as
5. the
6. east
7. is
8. from
9. the
10. west
11. that
12. is

SEED WORDS

13. how
14. far
15. away
16. our
17. heavenly
18. father
19. has
20. removed
21. our
22. sins
23. from
24. us

DAILY SEED

Wallet name
November 3

Derivation path
ot/proverbs/21/15

SEED WORDS

1. justice
2. brings
3. joy
4. to
5. the
6. righteous
7. but
8. terror
9. to
10. those
11. who
12. do

Passphrase: evil

DAILY SEED

Wallet name
November 4

Derivation path
ot/isaiah/10/1

SEED WORDS

1. woe
2. to
3. those
4. who
5. enact
6. evil
7. statutes
8. and
9. constantly
10. record
11. unjust
12. decisions

DAILY SEED

Wallet name
November 5

Derivation path
ot/proverbs/29/2

SEED WORDS

1. when
2. the
3. righteous
4. increase
5. the
6. people
7. rejoice
8. when
9. the
10. wicked
11. rule
12. people

Passphrase: _groan_

Wallet name
November 6

Derivation path
ot/proverbs/14/34

SEED WORDS

1. righteousness
2. exalts
3. a
4. nation
5. but
6. sin
7. is
8. a
9. reproach
10. to
11. any
12. people

Wallet name
November 7

Derivation path
ot/2chronicles/7/14

SEED WORDS

1. if
2. my
3. people
4. humble
5. themselves
6. seek
7. my
8. face
9. turn
10. from
11. wickedness
12. i

SEED WORDS

13. will
14. hear
15. from
16. heaven
17. and
18. forgive
19. their
20. sin
21. and
22. heal
23. their
24. land

Wallet name
November 8

Derivation path
ot/proverbs/28/15

SEED WORDS

1. like
2. roaring
3. lion
4. or
5. rushing
6. bear
7. is
8. wicked
9. ruler
10. over
11. the
12. poor

DAILY SEED

Wallet name
November 9

Derivation path
ot/1samuel/8/7

SEED WORDS

1. and
2. they
3. said
4. give
5. us
6. a
7. king
8. to
9. lead
10. us
11. and
12. the

SEED WORDS

13. lord
14. said
15. to
16. samuel
17. it
18. is
19. not
20. you
21. they
22. rejected
23. but
24. me

DAILY SEED

Wallet name
November 10

Derivation path
nt/romans/15/4

SEED WORDS

1. for
2. whatever
3. was
4. written
5. in
6. former
7. days
8. was
9. written
10. for
11. our
12. instruction

Wallet name
November 11

Derivation path
ot/proverbs/28/6

SEED WORDS

1. better
2. to
3. be
4. poor
5. with
6. integrity
7. than
8. to
9. be
10. crooked
11. and
12. rich

DAILY SEED

Wallet name
November 12

Derivation path
nt/luke/3/11

SEED WORDS

1. the
2. man
3. who
4. has
5. two
6. tunics
7. is
8. to
9. share
10. with
11. him
12. who

SEED WORDS

13. has
14. none
15. and
16. the
17. man
18. who
19. has
20. food
21. is
22. to
23. do
24. likewise

324

Wallet name
November 13

Derivation path
ot/micah/7/7

SEED WORDS

1. but
2. as
3. for
4. me
5. i
6. will
7. watch
8. in
9. hope
10. for
11. the
12. lord

DAILY SEED

Wallet name
November 14

Derivation path
nt/romans/12/12

SEED WORDS

1. rejoice
2. in
3. hope
4. be
5. patient
6. in
7. tribulation
8. and
9. be
10. constant
11. in
12. prayer

Wallet name
November 15

Derivation path
nt/galatians/5/22

SEED WORDS

1. but
2. the
3. fruit
4. of
5. the
6. spirit
7. is
8. love
9. joy
10. peace
11. forebearance
12. kindness

SEED WORDS

13. goodness
14. faithfulness
15. gentleness
16. and
17. self-control
18. against
19. such
20. things
21. there
22. is
23. no
24. law

DAILY SEED

Wallet name
November 16

Derivation path
nt/1peter/2/22

SEED WORDS

1. he
2. comitted
3. no
4. sin
5. nor
6. was
7. any
8. deceit
9. found
10. in
11. his
12. mouth

Wallet name
November 17

Derivation path
ot/psalm/107/2-3

SEED WORDS

1. let
2. the
3. redeemed
4. of
5. the
6. lord
7. tell
8. their
9. story
10. those
11. he
12. redeemed

SEED WORDS

13. from
14. the
15. hand
16. of
17. the
18. enemy
19. he
20. gathered
21. from
22. the
23. whole
24. Earth

Wallet name
November 18

Derivation path
ot/psalm/139/13-14

SEED WORDS

1. for
2. you
3. created
4. my
5. inmost
6. being
7. you
8. knit
9. me
10. together
11. in
12. my

SEED WORDS

13. mother's
14. womb
15. i
16. praise
17. you
18. because
19. i
20. am
21. fearfully
22. and
23. wonderfully
24. made

Wallet name
November 19

Derivation path
nt/matthew/6/33

SEED WORDS

1. but
2. seek
3. you
4. first
5. the
6. kingdom
7. of
8. God
9. and
10. his
11. righteousness
12. and

SEED WORDS

13. then
14. all
15. these
16. other
17. things
18. will
19. be
20. given
21. to
22. you
23. as
24. well

DAILY SEED

Wallet name
November 20

Derivation path
nt/matthew/13/45

SEED WORDS

1. the
2. kingdom
3. of
4. heaven
5. is
6. like
7. a
8. merchant
9. searching
10. for
11. pearls
12. when

SEED WORDS

13. he
14. found
15. one
16. of
17. great
18. value
19. he
20. sold
21. everything
22. to
23. buy
24. it

Wallet name
November 21

Derivation path
ot/proverbs/22/6

SEED WORDS

1. train
2. up
3. a
4. child
5. in
6. the
7. way
8. he
9. should
10. go
11. and
12. even

SEED WORDS

13. when
14. he
15. is
16. old
17. he
18. will
19. not
20. turn
21. away
22. from
23. his
24. training

Wallet name
November 22

Derivation path
ot/proverbs/22/16

SEED WORDS

1. whoever
2. oppresses
3. the
4. poor
5. to
6. make
7. more
8. for
9. himself
10. will
11. come
12. to

Passphrase: poverty

Wallet name
November 23

Derivation path
ot/jeremiah/5/27-28

SEED WORDS

1. their
2. houses
3. are
4. full
5. of
6. deceit
7. they
8. have
9. become
10. great
11. and
12. rich

SEED WORDS

13. they
14. do
15. not
16. defend
17. the
18. rights
19. of
20. the
21. orphan
22. or
23. the
24. poor

Wallet name
November 24

Derivation path
nt/john/6/55-56

SEED WORDS

1. my
2. flesh
3. is
4. food
5. and
6. my
7. blood
8. is
9. drink
10. whoever
11. eats
12. my

SEED WORDS

13. flesh
14. and
15. drinks
16. my
17. blood
18. remains
19. in
20. me
21. and
22. i
23. in
24. them

Wallet name
November 25

Derivation path
ot/jeremiah/27/11

SEED WORDS

1. like
2. a
3. partrich
4. that
5. hatches
6. eggs
7. that
8. are
9. not
10. its
11. own
12. so

SEED WORDS

13. is
14. he
15. who
16. makes
17. a
18. fortune
19. unjustly
20. off
21. the
22. work
23. of
24. others

DAILY SEED

Wallet name
November 26

Derivation path
ot/psalm/103/17

SEED WORDS

1. but
2. the
3. mercy
4. of
5. the
6. lord
7. is
8. from
9. everlasting
10. to
11. everlasting
12. on

SEED WORDS

13. those
14. who
15. love
16. him
17. and
18. his
19. righteousness
20. with
21. their
22. children
23. and
24. grandchildren

338

Wallet name
November 27

Derivation path
ot/proverbs/27/24

SEED WORDS

1. riches
2. do
3. not
4. last
5. forever
6. nor
7. a
8. crown
9. endure
10. for
11. all
12. generations

DAILY SEED

Wallet name
November 28

Derivation path
nt/acts/2/47

SEED WORDS

1. and
2. the
3. lord
4. added
5. to
6. their
7. number
8. daily
9. those
10. who
11. were
12. being

II

Passphrase: saved

Wallet name
November 29

Derivation path
nt/james/2/6

SEED WORDS

1. why
2. have
3. you
4. dishonored
5. the
6. poor
7. man
8. is
9. it
10. not
11. the
12. rich

SEED WORDS

13. and
14. the
15. wealthy
16. who
17. oppress
18. you
19. and
20. personally
21. drag
22. you
23. into
24. court

Wallet name
November 30

Derivation path
nt/1timothy/6/7

SEED WORDS

1. we
2. brought
3. nothing
4. into
5. this
6. world
7. we
8. can
9. take
10. nothing
11. from
12. it

DAILY SEED

Wallet name
December 1

Derivation path
ot/genesis/3/6

SEED WORDS

1. she
2. took
3. the
4. fruit
5. and
6. ate
7. as
8. did
9. her
10. husband
11. with
12. her

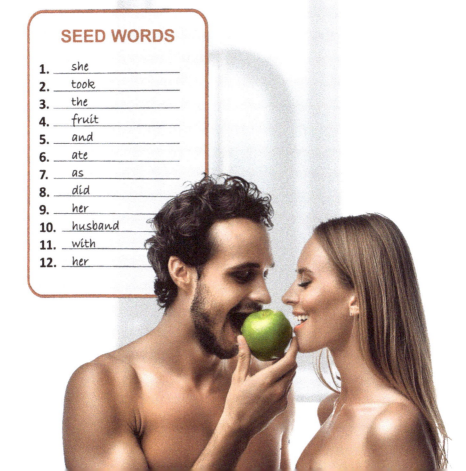

Wallet name
December 2

Derivation path
ot/psalm/51/3

SEED WORDS

1. for
2. i
3. know
4. my
5. transgressions
6. and
7. my
8. sin
9. is
10. always
11. before
12. me

Wallet name
December 3

Derivation path
nt/1john/4/15

SEED WORDS

1. if
2. anyone
3. acknowledges
4. jesus
5. is
6. the
7. son
8. of
9. God
10. God
11. lives
12. in

Passphrase: them

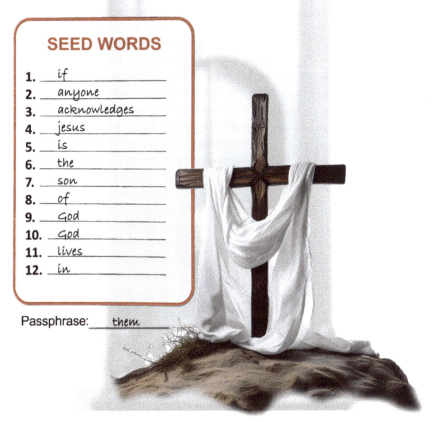

345

DAILY SEED

Wallet name
December 4

Derivation path
ot/psalm/42/5

SEED WORDS

1. why
2. my
3. soul
4. are
5. you
6. downcast
7. why
8. so
9. disturbed
10. within
11. me
12. put

SEED WORDS

13. your
14. hope
15. in
16. God
17. for
18. i
19. will
20. yet
21. praise
22. him
23. my
24. savior

346

Wallet name
December 5

Derivation path
nt/john/10/10

SEED WORDS

1. the
2. thief
3. comes
4. to
5. steal
6. kill
7. destroy
8. but
9. i
10. came
11. to
12. give

Passphrase: life

Wallet name
December 6

Derivation path
ot/psalm/110/1

SEED WORDS

1. the
2. lord
3. said
4. to
5. my
6. lord
7. sit
8. here
9. at
10. my
11. right
12. hand

SEED WORDS

13. in
14. honor
15. until
16. i
17. make
18. your
19. enemies
20. a
21. footstool
22. for
23. your
24. feet

Wallet name
December 7

Derivation path
ot/psalm/105/2

SEED WORDS

1. sing
2. to
3. him
4. sing
5. praise
6. to
7. him
8. tell
9. of
10. his
11. wonderful
12. acts

DAILY SEED

Wallet name
December 8

Derivation path
nt/james/4/7

SEED WORDS

1. submit
2. to
3. God
4. resist
5. the
6. devil
7. and
8. he
9. will
10. flee
11. from
12. you

350

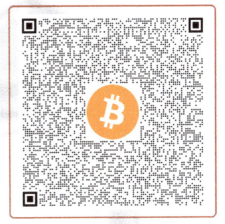

DAILY SEED

Wallet name
December 9

Derivation path
ot/psalm/40/16

SEED WORDS

1. may
2. all
3. who
4. seek
5. you
6. rejoice
7. and
8. be
9. glad
10. in
11. you
12. those

SEED WORDS

13. who
14. long
15. for
16. your
17. saving
18. help
19. always
20. say
21. the
22. lord
23. is
24. great

Wallet name
December 10

Derivation path
nt/john/6/67-68

SEED WORDS

1. jesus
2. asked
3. them
4. do
5. you
6. want
7. to
8. leave
9. too
10. peter
11. answered
12. to

SEED WORDS

13. whom
14. shall
15. we
16. go
17. only
18. you
19. have
20. the
21. words
22. of
23. eternal
24. life

352

DAILY SEED

Wallet name
December 11

Derivation path
nt/matthew/11/28'30

SEED WORDS

1. come
2. to
3. me
4. you
5. who
6. are
7. weary
8. and
9. burdened
10. i
11. will
12. give

SEED WORDS

13. you
14. rest
15. for
16. my
17. yoke
18. is
19. easy
20. and
21. my
22. burden
23. is
24. light

353

DAILY SEED

Wallet name
December 12

Derivation path
nt/matthew/13/54

SEED WORDS

1. where
2. did
3. jesus
4. get
5. this
6. wisdom
7. and
8. these
9. miraculous
10. powers
11. they
12. asked

354

Wallet name
December 13

Derivation path
nt/luke/18/24

SEED WORDS

1. it
2. is
3. hard
4. for
5. the
6. rich
7. to
8. enter
9. the
10. kingdom
11. of
12. God

DAILY SEED

Wallet name
December 14

Derivation path
ot/psalm/118/24

SEED WORDS

1. this
2. is
3. a
4. day
5. the
6. lord
7. made
8. rejoice
9. be
10. glad
11. in
12. it

Wallet name
December 15

Derivation path
nt/matthew/7/28

SEED WORDS

1. when
2. jesus
3. finished
4. saying
5. these
6. things
7. the
8. crowd
9. marveled
10. at
11. his
12. teaching

DAILY SEED

Wallet name
December 16

Derivation path
ot/proverbs/29/5

SEED WORDS

1. a
2. man
3. who
4. flatters
5. his
6. neighbor
7. is
8. spreading
9. a
10. net
11. for
12. his

Passphrase: _steps_

358

Wallet name
December 17

Derivation path
ot/isaiah/65/1

SEED WORDS

1. i
2. revealed
3. myself
4. to
5. those
6. who
7. did
8. not
9. even
10. look
11. for
12. me

SEED WORDS

13. and
14. i
15. was
16. found
17. by
18. those
19. who
20. did
21. not
22. seek
23. me
24. out

359

Wallet name
December 18

Derivation path
ot/lamentations/3/23

SEED WORDS

1. his
2. mercies
3. never
4. fail
5. they
6. are
7. new
8. every
9. morning
10. great
11. is
12. your

Passphrase: _faithfulness_

Wallet name
December 19

Derivation path
ot/proverbs/30/8

SEED WORDS

1. give
2. me
3. neither
4. poverty
5. nor
6. riches
7. but
8. give
9. only
10. my
11. daily
12. bread

Wallet name
December 20

Derivation path
ot/daniel/6/20

SEED WORDS

1. daniel
2. has
3. your
4. God
5. been
6. able
7. to
8. save
9. you
10. from
11. the
12. lions

DAILY SEED

SEED WORDS

1. vindicate
2. me
3. my
4. God
5. and
6. plead
7. my
8. case
9. against
10. an
11. unfaithful
12. nation

SEED WORDS

13. rescue
14. me
15. from
16. those
17. who
18. are
19. deceitful
20. and
21. wicked
22. you
23. are
24. God

DAILY SEED

Wallet name
December 22

Derivation path
ot/micah/5/2

SEED WORDS

1. Bethlehem
2. Ephrathah
3. though
4. you
5. are
6. small
7. among
8. the
9. clans
10. of
11. judah
12. out

SEED WORDS

13. of
14. you
15. will
16. come
17. one
18. who
19. will
20. be
21. ruler
22. over
23. my
24. people

364

Wallet name
December 23

Derivation path
ot/isaiah/9/6a

SEED WORDS

1. for
2. unto
3. us
4. a
5. child
6. is
7. born
8. for
9. unto
10. us
11. a
12. son

SEED WORDS

13. is
14. given
15. and
16. he
17. alone
18. shall
19. carry
20. the
21. government
22. on
23. his
24. shoulders

Wallet name
December 24

Derivation path
ot/isaiah/9/6b

SEED WORDS

1. his
2. name
3. is
4. wonderful
5. counselor
6. mighty
7. God
8. everlasting
9. father
10. prince
11. of
12. peace

366

Wallet name
December 25

Derivation path
nt/luke/2/11

SEED WORDS

1. for
2. there
3. is
4. born
5. to
6. you
7. this
8. day
9. in
10. the
11. town
12. of

SEED WORDS

13. david
14. a
15. savior
16. he
17. is
18. the
19. messiah
20. who
21. is
22. christ
23. the
24. lord

367

DAILY SEED

Wallet name
December 26

Derivation path
nt/matthew/8/27

SEED WORDS

1. who
2. can
3. this
4. be
5. that
6. even
7. the
8. wind
9. and
10. waves
11. obey
12. him

368

Wallet name
December 27

Derivation path
nt/matthew/14/14

SEED WORDS

1. when
2. jesus
3. saw
4. the
5. crowd
6. he
7. had
8. compassion
9. and
10. healed
11. their
12. sick

369

Wallet name
December 28

Derivation path
nt/john/12/46

SEED WORDS

1. jesus
2. proclaimed
3. i
4. have
5. come
6. as
7. a
8. light
9. into
10. the
11. world
12. so

SEED WORDS

13. that
14. no
15. one
16. who
17. believes
18. in
19. me
20. should
21. remain
22. in
23. the
24. darkness

Wallet name
December 29

Derivation path
nt/revelation/5/2

SEED WORDS

1. who
2. is
3. there
4. worthy
5. to
6. break
7. the
8. seal
9. and
10. open
11. the
12. scroll

Wallet name
December 30

Derivation path
nt/revelation/22/3

SEED WORDS

1. there
2. shall
3. be
4. no
5. more
6. curse
7. the
8. throne
9. of
10. god
11. and
12. the

SEED WORDS

13. lamb
14. shall
15. be
16. in
17. the
18. city
19. and
20. his
21. servants
22. will
23. serve
24. him

Wallet name
December 31

Derivation path
nt/revelation/22/13

SEED WORDS

1. i
2. am
3. the
4. alpha
5. and
6. the
7. omega
8. the
9. beginning
10. and
11. the
12. end

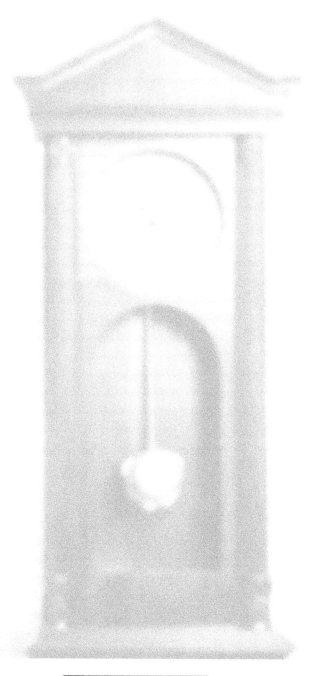

ABOUT THE AUTHOR

Daniel Howell is a professor at Liberty University where he teaches human anatomy to nursing and premed students. He joined the LU faculty in 2003 after spending six years conducting biomedical research at Duke University and McGill University.

Dr. Howell discovered Bitcoin in the fall of 2020. Like so many others, he was dismayed by the money printing for COVID 'stimi checks' and wondered how that worked. For the first time, he asked, 'what is money?' and discovered that the dollar is a fiat currency Ponzi scheme. Bitcoin seemed promising, so he ventured down the rabbit hole, bought his first sats, and never looked back.

You can follow Daniel on Twitter or Nostr using the QR codes below.

nostr npub for Dr. Daniel Howell (HashBros)

@drdanielhowell

Terms Used in the Daily Seed

$5 wrench attack: being physically attacked to steal your bitcoins.
Anon: anonymous.
Anti-fragile: the phenomenon of getting stronger when attacked.
ATH: all-time-high.
Cantillon effect: the financial advantage that those with a close relationship with central banks have over those who do not.
CBDC: central bank digital currency.
Cold storage: the most secure way to store your bitcoins; a cold wallet is one that is never connected to the internet; a hot wallet is one that does connect to the internet.
DCA: dollar cost average; daily buying bitcoin.
Diamond hands: a strong resolve to hold your bitcoin stack despite pressure to sell. Opposite lettuce hands.
Faucet: a website that gives away free bitcoins.
FUD: fear, uncertainty, and doubt.
God candle: a rapid rise in Bitcoin's price.
Hard fork: a change in the Bitcoin protocol.
HODL: a misspelling of HOLD; to not sell your bitcoin stack.
Honey badger don't care: having little regard for market sentiment.
KYC/AML: know your customer/anti-money laundering laws.
LARP: live action role playing.
Lettuce hands: having a weak will; selling your bitcoin for fear of getting rekt. Opposite diamond hands.
Money-printer-go-brrr: the creation of money out of thin air by the federal reserve central bank.
NGMI: not gonna make it.
NGU: number go up; the Bitcoin price is going up forever.
Pleb: Plebian; a commoner.
Proof-of-work: the protocol used by Bitcoin to secure the blockchain.
Rekt: losing lots of money.
Sats: abbreviation for Satoshis; the smallest unit of bitcoin.
SBF: Sam Bankman-Fried; a thief.
Shipcoin: any cryptocurrency other than Bitcoin; a polite spin on shitcoin.
Stack: your bitcoin holdings.
Tick-tock-next-block: nothing stops Bitcoin; every 10 minutes a new block will be added to the blockchain no matter what is happening in politics, the financial markets, or otherwise.
W: win; opposite L (lose).